© 1995 by MorningStar Publications, Inc. All Rights Reserved.

*Editor: Rick Joyner*
*Contributing Editors: Jack Deere, Francis Frangipane and Dudley Hall*
*General Editor: Steve Thompson*
*Managing Editor: Dianne C. Thomas*
*Production Manager: Mike Chaille*
*Production Assistant: Roger Hedgspeth*
*Copy Editors: Becky Chaille, Terri Herrera*

**The Morning Star Journal** is published quarterly, 4 issues per year, by MorningStar Publications, Inc., 16000 Lancaster Hwy, Charlotte, NC 28277-2061. Summer-1995 issue. Second-class postage pending, Charlotte, NC and additional mailing offices.

POSTMASTER: Send address corrections to **The Morning Star Journal**, 16000 Lancaster Hwy, Charlotte, NC 28277-2061. Subscription Rates: One year $12.95. Outside U.S. $20.00.

*MorningStar Publications* is a non-profit organization dedicated to the promulgation of important teachings and timely prophetic messages to the church. We also attempt to promote interchange between the different streams, emphases and denominations in the body of Christ.

**To receive a subscription** to *The Morning Star Journal,* send payment along with your name and address to MorningStar Publications, 16000 Lancaster Hwy, Charlotte, NC 28277-2061, (704) 542-0278 (1-800-542-0278—**Orders only**); FAX (704) 542-0280. One year (4 quarterly issues) U.S. $12.95; outside U.S. $20.00. Prices are subject to change without notice.

**Reprints.** Photocopies of any part of the contents of this publication may be made freely. However, to re-typeset information, permission must be requested in writing from MorningStar Publications, 16000 Lancaster Hwy, Charlotte, NC 28277-2061.

**Letters.** Direct all correspondence to the address above. Contributions are tax deductible. Your support is appreciated.

*In this Journal* NAS *refers to the New American Standard Bible, copyright © 1960, 1962, 1963, 1968, 1971, 1973, 1974, 1977, by The Lockman Foundation.* NKJV *refers to the Holy Bible, New King James Version, © 1979, 1980, 1982 by Thomas Nelson, Inc.* NIV *refers to Holy Bible: New International Version ®, NIV®, © 1973, 1978, 1984 by International Bible Society.* AMP *refers to The Amplified Bible, © 1954, 1958, 1962, 1964, 1965 by Zondervan Publishing House.* RSV *refers to The Revised Standard Version, © 1962 by The World Publishing Co.* TLB *refers to The Living Bible © 1971 by Tyndale House Publishers.* ASV *refers to the American Standard Version. Italics in Scripture references are for emphasis only.*

# WRESTLING WITH PRINCIPALITIES

by

## Rick Joyner

*All Scriptures NAS unless otherwise indicated.*

**Finally, be strong in the Lord, and in the strength of His might.**

**Put on the full armor of God, that you may be able to stand firm against the schemes of the devil.**

**For our struggle is not against flesh and blood, but against the rulers, against the powers, against the world forces of this darkness, against the spiritual forces of wickedness in the heavenly places.**

**Therefore, take up the full armor of God, that you may be able to resist in the evil day, and having done everything, to stand firm.**

**Stand firm therefore, having girded your loins with truth, and having put on the breastplate of righteousness,**

**and having shod your feet with the preparation of the gospel of peace;**

**in addition to all, taking up the shield of faith with which you will be able to extinguish all the flaming missiles of the evil one.**

**And take the helmet of salvation, and the sword of the Spirit, which is the word of God.**

**With all prayer and petition pray at all times in the Spirit, and with this in view, be on the alert with all perseverance and petition for all the saints (Ephesians 6:10-18).**

This text provides one of the basic outlines for spiritual warfare in Scripture. It begins with the most important point in our battle with evil:

**Finally, be strong in the Lord, and in the strength of His might (verse 10).**

We are fighting against a foe that is far more experienced, wiser and more powerful than we are. We will never win with our own intelligence, strength, goodness, or determination. To win this fight we must know and learn to stand in the strength of the Lord. As James stated it:

But He gives a greater grace. Therefore it says, "God is opposed to the proud, but gives grace to the humble."

Submit therefore to God. Resist the devil and he will flee from you.

Draw near to God and He will draw near to you (James 4:6-8).

Here we see that the exhortation to resist the devil is sandwiched between the exhortations to submit to God and to draw near to Him. The first step in spiritual warfare will always be toward God, not the devil. To be successful we must both submit to the Lord and draw near to Him.

In this text we also see that humility enables us to receive the grace of God, and the grace of God is a power much greater than that of any enemy. Those who walk in humility, which is submission to God, will see the devils fleeing from them. We are an easy prey for them when we depart from His grace by walking in pride, which is basically taking our stand based on our own strength or wisdom.

The enemy himself fell when he became prideful, and he knows very well that the first step in getting us to fall is to make us proud. **"Therefore let him who thinks he stands take heed lest he fall" (I Corinthians 10:12).** When we think that *we* are the ones who are standing, we will be in jeopardy of a fall. But when we take our stand on the grace of God and the victory of Jesus Christ, all the hordes of hell will not be able to bring us down. True humility is to stand on the finished work of Christ, alone!

Put on the *full* armor of God, that you may be able to stand

firm against the schemes of the devil (Ephesians 6:11).

We are in a battle. We must be protected or we will be wounded. Many have presumed that because they have submitted themselves to God that He will protect them. Of course, the Lord protects His people, but one way that He does this is by giving us the armor to put on. If we do not wear what He has provided for our protection we are not submitting to Him, but are walking in a foolish presumption, which is pride, which in turn removes us from the grace upon which we stand.

The immature or insecure often become fearful when confronted with responsibility. However, with redemption comes an awesome responsibility to this lost world. Adam did not seem to understand that his fall would result in such unfathomable tragedy for billions of souls. Few church leaders realize that when they fall they will drag down many of those that our Savior entrusted to their keeping. Along with the authority to be joint heirs with the Son of God, He has also delegated to us a very real responsibility.

Immediately after His resurrection the Lord had the legal right to bind or destroy Satan and reclaim this earth. Why did He not do it? For our sake! The entire church age was for the bride to prove her devotion and faithfulness by overcoming a world that is in the grips of evil, and to learn the responsibility that will enable her to reign with Christ. This whole age is a test. God's tests are not given so that we can fail, but so that we can be promoted. This life is a test to see where each of us can be placed in the authority of His eternal kingdom.

There is an aspect of battle when real issues, even life and death, are decided, and the essence of who we are surfaces. Will we selfishly hide and hoard our salvation, or will we fight for truth and righteousness? Will we lead others into the life of the Son of God, or will we give way to sin and rebellion under pressure, and drag others down with us? Now, at the culmination of this age, when the deepest darkness of all is coming upon the earth, there will be the greatest conflict between good and evil. We must pick up our armor and fight. We may die fighting for the kingdom, or we may be caught up in the air, but let us be caught up while attacking with unyielding resolution the darkness of our times, and using our shields of faith for the protection of the weak or immature.

## There Are No "Time-Outs" in Battle

The exhortation is to put on the "full" armor. If we leave off part of our protection the enemy will very likely find it, and he will hit us there. There are no truces in this conflict—we cannot just say that we are tired and do not want to fight anymore for awhile. We cannot say, "Don't hit me in that place." Our enemy will not play by our rules, and he will not play fair. He is looking for anything that he can use to exploit. We must therefore be careful not to take our armor off, or to lay down our shield of faith.

The Scriptures are full of examples of men who left a small opening in their life only to have the enemy flooding through the gap. King David's great sin is an obvious example. In the spring, **"when kings go out to battle" (II Samuel 11:1),** he stayed home. The result was that he fell into adultery and committed murder to cover it up in one of the most tragic falls from grace in the Scriptures. The Lord forgave him, but the sword did not depart from his house until tragedy struck some of his own family. The Lord will forgive our sins, but there will still be consequences for them—we will reap what we sow, and those entrusted to our care will suffer.

Just as David learned, when it is time to fight, one of the most dangerous places that we can be is in the rear. When the enemy sees us dropping back or letting up, he will hit us even harder. Never forget that our enemy has no mercy or compassion, and he is determined to destroy us. However, he has no power against us as long as we are submitted to the Lord, drawing closer to Him, and resisting the devil; but we must do all three.

## Higher Levels, Bigger Devils

The more spiritual authority we have, and the more of a threat that we are to the enemy, the more of a target we will be. The enemy did not just send a principality to tempt Jesus, or to sift Peter, he trusted them to no one but himself. The more spiritual authority that we have, the greater our opposition will be. Conversely, the greater our opposition, when we have effectively resisted, the greater the evil that will be fleeing from us. Many fall because they do not understand this, and with increased spiritual authority they begin to relax their vigilance rather than increase it. This is one reason why so many tragically fall at the end of their lives. It does not matter how many great miracles we have been used by God to perform, or how many souls we have led to salvation, or how many devils we have cast out; if we do not continue to submit to God, draw near to Him and resist the devil, we *will* be in jeopardy.

Satan himself accuses the saints before the throne of God; therefore, the closer we get to the throne, the higher the level of accusation we will be bombarded with. The Lord could stop this at any time, but He allows it for our maturity, and also for the bringing down of the higher levels of evil principalities. Remember how the evil spirit answered the Jewish exorcists: **"Jesus I know, and Paul I know; but who are you?" (Acts 19:15 NKJV)?** All of hell knew Paul because of the level of authority he had been given, which is why he experienced continual opposition to his ministry. But, with each level of opposition, with each new beating, stoning, or persecution, he had the opportunity to drive out higher levels of darkness. This is why Paul said:

> **In no way alarmed by your opponents—which is a sign of destruction for them, but of salvation for you, and that too, from God.**
> **For to you it has been granted for Christ's sake, not only to believe in Him, but also to suffer for His sake (Philippians 1:28-29).**

Opposition is a sign that salvation is coming to that realm or circumstance. It is also a sign of destruction for the enemy in that region. It has been granted to us to suffer for Christ's sake *as a form of spiritual warfare*. The greatest act of spiritual warfare, which utterly defeated the enemy and spoiled his camp, was the cross. Righteous suffering disarms the enemy.

It is by the Lord's stripes that we are healed. In the very place that He was wounded, He received authority for healing. The same is true for us. In the very place that the enemy wounds us, when we are healed, we will receive authority for healing in that same area. In the place where we are wounded, even after we are healed, we will forever be sensitive. For example, a person who has suffered abuse will be sensitive to others who have been abused, and have authority for bringing healing to them.

## We must Take a Stand (Verse 11b)

This is the first strategy that we are given. To take a stand means that we refuse to give ground, that we will not retreat. It must be a settled issue that when the Lord calls us to a place we will not depart from it under pressure. We are not called to go from defeat to defeat, but from glory to glory. Only when we have attained the victory and the glory has come to a place should we ever leave it, and then we should only leave to go on to a higher level.

The Lord allows principalities to take dominion over an area, and remain, until the church rises up in the opposite spirit to displace them. For example, the principality over Northern Virginia is the spirit of division. I was shown in a vision that this power gained its authority during the Civil War battles where brother slew brother. The blood still cries out from the ground in that region. The first step to victory over this area will be for the church to take a stand for unity and against division. The enemy's obvious counterattack in this area will come from accusations, slander and faultfinding, which are meant to maintain or increase division. For the church there to stand it will have to grow in unity by showing mercy, for "mercy triumphs over judgment" (James 2:13). To show mercy is to show undeserved forgiveness or favor. Not taking into account wrongs suffered not only solidifies unity, but it also enables us to take ground from the spirit of division by growing in these great graces of the Holy Spirit.

A primary principality over Charlotte, North Carolina is "charismatic witchcraft." This title is not meant to denote Charismatics as a group, but rather "human charisma," that is used as a substitute for the anointing. In Charlotte, we must be on special guard against using hype, manipulation, or control while seeking to accomplish the purpose of God, and must fight constantly against the temptation. Because witchcraft is counterfeit spiritual authority, we must be diligent to seek the Lord for true spiritual authority, and take our stand on it.

**For we wrestle not against flesh and blood, but against principalities, against powers, against the rulers of the darkness of this world, against spiritual wickedness in high places (Ephesians 6:12 KJV).**

Wrestling is the very closest form of combat. We are in a very personal, eyeball to eyeball struggle with the enemy. Wrestling is a struggle in which each combatant seeks to gain a position of advantage over the other one. The first advantage that our enemy will gain over us is if we start warring against "flesh and blood," or people.

People, even those who the enemy is using, are never our enemy, but they are the ones we are seeking to set free. In the place of true spiritual maturity we should never even get mad at other people. When we do it is only because we are failing to recognize the reality of the situation—that we are not warring against people, but *for* them, against the powers of wickedness in the spiritual realm that are deceiving those people.

This is not to imply that every one who is contrary, or who attacks us, is being driven by demons. Most are not, they are just being fallen human beings and doing what fallen human beings do. But even in these circumstances we need to know that God is allowing this to come upon us so that we can grow. The only way we will grow in love is to learn to love the unlovable. The way we will grow in the peace of God is to abide in the peace of God when everything seems

> IF YOU ARE GOING TO SWING AT GOLIATH, YOU HAD BETTER BE ABLE TO HIT HIM IN THE HEAD WITH THE FIRST SHOT!

to be going wrong. The only way we will grow in patience is to be put in circumstances where we will need more of it.

**Therefore, take up the full armor of God, that you may be able to resist in the evil day, and having done everything, to stand firm (verse 13).**

This is a repetition of the previous exhortations. Whenever God repeats something it is to emphasize the seriousness of the matter. This is so that we might **"resist in the evil day."** We can count on evil being released in a greater way when we confront it. Satan will seldom give up territory without a fight. We see in Revelation 12:7-12 that when Satan is cast out of heaven he comes down to the earth with great wrath, knowing that he only has a short time. Every time Satan is displaced in the heavenly places he comes down with wrath. When he stirs up evil on the earth we should be encouraged, knowing that we are taking ground in the heavenly places. Many give up at this point, but it is not the time to retreat, but to press the attack.

**Stand firm therefore, having girded your loins with truth, and having put on the breastplate of righteousness (verse 14).**

Truth is not only an offensive weapon—when used as the sword of the Spirit—but is our protection also. Truth will never be defeated. It may have seeming setbacks, but it will always prevail. As Mahesh Chavda said, "For 70 years the communists declared that God was dead. Then one day the Lord declared that communism was dead! Now, all of the places where the communists declared

their doctrine from hell, there is the greatest hunger for the word of God!"

The church is called to be "the pillar and support of the truth." When we compromise truth we compromise the very foundation of what we are called to be. The utter commitment to truth is a strong foundation and protection from the onslaught of the enemy, who is the **"father of lies."** Truth is more powerful than a lie, just as light is more powerful than darkness. When you open your shades at night, darkness does not come in; the light shines into the darkness because it is more powerful.

The breastplate guards the heart. Our righteousness is to be right with God, which is to be found in Jesus. As long as we are abiding in Him there is no weapon that can touch our heart.

**Having shod your feet with the preparation of the gospel of peace (verse 15).**

We walk with our feet, and if we have properly put on the armor of God, we will walk in peace. The peace of God is not only effective protection against the enemy, but it is also a powerful offensive weapon as we use our feet to crush the head of the serpent.

It is not the "Lord of Hosts," or "Lord of Armies" that crushes the enemy, but **"the God of Peace will soon crush Satan under your feet" (Romans 16:20).** We must be careful not to let anything steal our peace, or we will be deprived of a most important protection and weapon.

**In addition to all, taking up the shield of faith with which you**

**will be able to extinguish all of the flaming missiles of the evil one (Ephesians 6:16).**

The faith that we have been given is a shield that can extinguish anything that the enemy throws at us. If we are getting wounded, it is because we have dropped our faith. Pick up the shield!

Everyone in the fight is going to have flaming missiles thrown at them. The issue is, are we going to be hit with them, or are we going to be able to extinguish them. Faith is not to keep us from coming under attack, but rather to extinguish what the enemy throws at us.

**And take the helmet of salvation, and the sword of the Spirit, which is the word of God (verse 17).**

The helmet of salvation is for protecting our minds. It is easy to relax and take off our helmets, letting the pollution of the world attack our minds from TV, magazines, or in daily life. We must be vigilant to always guard our minds or we will open ourselves to potentially fatal head wounds that are intended to rob us of our salvation. The helmet is our salvation and we must wear it continually.

The sword is a defensive weapon, but it is also the chief offensive weapon, and our sword is the word of God. When Jesus was attacked by the devil, He used the word of God to drive him off. How much more should we learn to use this most powerful weapon? The more knowledge that we have of the word of God, the more skillful we will be in spiritual warfare, and the more effective we will be in attacking the strongholds of the enemy.

## After the Armor

The next step in spiritual warfare is stated in verse 18:

**With all prayer and petition pray at all times in the Spirit, and with this in view, be on the alert with all perseverance and petition for all the saints.**

What is the first purpose of intercession given here? **"For all the saints."** Our first priority is not to try to beat down principalities, but to pray for the saints to be strengthened.

For example, ministries based in the city of Charlotte have been used to humiliate the international body of Christ, which was the fruit of the "charismatic witchcraft" that had gained a foothold here. Our response was not to try to pray down that principality, but to pray for the Lord to raise up a standard of true spiritual authority here, and that the church be delivered from attempting to build on pride and manipulation, which will always bring God's resistance and a fall. We constantly pray for the Lord to strengthen the saints in the area that is the counterpoint to the enemy's strategy.

When we do pray for the Lord to bind the enemy, or cast him out of a region, we must not **"box in such a way, as not beating the air" (I Corinthians 9:26).** If you are going to swing at Goliath, you had better be able to hit him in the head with the first shot! Then you had better take his head off while you have him down. To hit him in the head means to clearly identify the principality. David used Goliath's own sword to cut off his head. The sword of the enemy is the enemy's word against the saints, just as the sword of the Lord is His word for the saints. When the enemy said that the church in Charlotte is built only on hype, manipulation and soul power, the church began to rise up with great resolve to walk in true spiritual authority, using what was meant as a curse and turning it into a call for action.

I have not yet personally witnessed the church in a locality that yet had the authority to actually cast down a principality. The gates of hell cannot prevail against the church (singular), but it will prevail against churches (plural). That is, the powers of hell cannot prevail against the church in unity, but they can prevail over churches that are divided. It will take a citywide church to establish city-wide spiritual authority. A local congregation that is in unity may be able to take some spiritual authority over its own neighborhood, but it is most unlikely that it will have any impact over the whole city.

It is not wise for individual saints, and even individual congregations, to go to war against a principality over their region until they are in unity with the rest of the church in that region. That is why we must first pray to **"strengthen the saints"** against the strategy or influence of the enemy in that region. When the church becomes strong enough in the strength of the Lord to take spiritual dominion, it will also be able to hold out against the counterattack that always comes. Whenever a demon is cast out, on any level, it does say, **"I will return" (Matthew 12:44** NIV**).**

## Spoiling and Disarming the Enemy

To spoil the enemy is to take what is in his possession. This should be our primary goal in spiritual warfare. We should ask the Lord for specific targets, such as the youth in our city, certain neighborhoods, the city council, the press, etc., which may now be in the control of the enemy, and begin a concentrated prayer assault until they are in the hands of the Lord. In this text, Colossians 2:8-23, the Lord gives us a step-by-step procedure for doing this:

> **See to it that no one takes you captive through philosophy and empty deception, according to the tradition of men, according to the elementary principles of the world, rather than according to Christ (verse 8).**

Beware of philosophies, for they are meant to distract us from the only true source of our power—the cross and the word of God. When the enemy knows that we are going to fight for our city or region, one of his strategies is to send in humanistic philosophies that seem to seek the same thing that we are seeking. This is a distraction that will knock us from our course and deprive us of the victory!

> **For in Him all the fulness of Deity dwells in bodily form (verse 9).**

Our warfare must be waged on "Christ plus nothing." He is enough! One of the greatest traps of the enemy in our time has been to get the church to try to wage war against the spiritual powers of darkness using psychology and other philosophical solutions. Every one of these that the world has tried to implement has only resulted in greater darkness and despair. Why does the church not learn that man will never have the answers to his problems unless he goes to the cross?

**And in Him you have been made complete, and He is the head over all rule and authority (verse 10).**

We must never be moved from the position that the cross and the word of God alone have the answers to human problems! Being complete in Him also means that we include the entire body of Christ in our region. In all of our conflict we must remember that He is the Head over all rule and authority, and He will not let the enemy do anything to us that does not accomplish His purposes, just as it was only by the authority of the Father that Pontius Pilate had authority to crucify the Lord. We must not trust in what we see on earth, but in the One who is above the earth, and all powers in the earth.

**And in Him you were also circumcised with a circumcision made without hands, in the removal of the body of the flesh by the circumcision of Christ (verse 11).**

We can count on our flesh being cut away by our confrontations with the enemy. Let us not resist this work, but embrace it for our own growth, which will result in our being made trustworthy for even more authority (which will mean more battles, etc.).

**Having been buried with Him in baptism, in which you were also raised up with Him through faith in the working of God, who raised Him from the dead (verse 12).**

To be baptized is to die with Christ, which means that we must be dead to this world and the forces of this world, that we might walk in resurrection power. What can the enemy or the world do to a dead man? If we are dead to this world it can do nothing to us. It is impossible for a dead man to feel rejection, fear, insults, etc. Like the apostle Paul, if we commit ourselves to spoil the strongman we must be ready to take the stripes upon our own back.

**And when you were dead in your transgressions and the uncircumcision of your flesh, He made you alive together with Him, having forgiven us all our transgressions (verse 13).**

We can count on the accuser releasing everything that he can against us, especially dragging up our own sins in the area that we are now seeking to displace him. Here we must take our stand on the forgiveness of God, and the knowledge that we are not coming in our own righteousness, but the Lord's. We have been promised that if we have died with Him we will also be raised with Him—the resurrection is true! Regardless of what the enemy does to us, glory and resurrection power will ultimately result!

**Having canceled out the certificate of debt consisting of decrees against us and which was hostile**

**to us; and He has taken it out of the way, having nailed it to the cross (verse 14).**

This is again the exhortation to focus on the only power that will win the victory, the cross of Jesus, alone upon which we take our stand. Remember, when the Lord repeats a matter it is to emphasize the seriousness of it.

**When He had disarmed the rulers and authorities, He made a public display of them, having triumphed over them through Him (verse 15).**

We must expect the battle to be public if the victory is to be for the whole city or region. This is why all of Jerusalem first worshiped the Lord, then denied and rejected Him. Everyone was involved, so that everyone could potentially benefit. We see this also with the apostle Paul's confrontation with idolatry in Ephesus, intellectualism in Athens, and the religious spirit in Jerusalem. In each case the whole city was stirred. This is because the highest level of evil powers in that region had been threatened and agitated.

**Therefore let no one act as your judge in regard to food or drink or in respect to a festival or a new moon, or a Sabbath day—**

**things which are a mere shadow of what is to come; but the substance belongs to Christ (verses 16-17).**

Our enemy's name is, "Accuser of the brethren," because that is what he is best at, getting brothers to accuse one another. The accusations listed above are all in relation to religious requirements or events, which would only come from religious people—our brothers.

It is hard for Christians to realize that most of the opposition that will come to those who are making a spiritual advance will come from other Christians. This was true in the first century church, as the converts from among the Pharisees became the greatest enemies of the gospel of God's grace, and it has been true of every spiritual generation since. If we are going to make a spiritual advance we must learn to do so while suffering counterattacks from both the front and the rear.

**Let no one keep defrauding you of your prize by delighting in self-abasement and the worship of the angels, taking his stand on visions he has seen, inflated without cause by his fleshly mind,**

**and not holding fast to the head, from whom the entire body, being supplied and held together by the joints and ligaments, grows with a growth which is from God.**

**If you have died with Christ to the elementary principles of the world, why, as if you were living in the world, do you submit yourself to decrees, such as,**

**"Do not handle, do not taste, do not touch!"**

**(which all refer to things destined to perish with the using)—in accordance with the commandments and teachings of men?**

**These are matters which have, to be sure, the appearance of wisdom in self-made religion and**

self-abasement and severe treatment of the body, but are of no value against fleshly indulgence (Colossians 2:18-23).

The greatest assault on every move of God will come from the religious spirit, which we must recognize and reject. (This subject is addressed in depth in the article entitled "The Religious Spirit," in *The Morning Star Journal, Volume Five, Number One,* and is also addressed in the book, *Epic Battles of the Last Days.*)

If then you have been raised up with Christ, keep seeking the things above, where Christ is, seated at the right hand of God.

Set your mind on the things above, not on the things that are on earth.

For you have died and your life is hidden with Christ in God.

When Christ, who is our life, is revealed, then you also will be revealed with Him in glory (Colossians 3:1-4).

Throughout every battle we must keep our attention on the Lord, not the enemy. Our victory comes from abiding in Christ, and following Him.

## Apostolic Preaching as Spiritual Warfare

To me, the very least of all saints, this grace was given, to preach to the Gentiles the unfathomable riches of Christ,

and to bring to light what is the administration of the mystery which for ages has been hidden in God, who created all things;

in order that the manifold wisdom of God might now be made known through the church to the rulers and the authorities in the heavenly places (Ephesians 3:8-10).

The apostles did not cast down principalities by yelling at them, or even addressing them directly, but by confronting their power with their lives and messages. As Jude stated it:

But Michael the archangel, when he disputed with the devil and argued about the body of Moses, did not dare pronounce against him a railing judgment, but said, "The Lord rebuke you."

But these men revile the things which they do not understand; and the things which they know by instinct, like unreasoning animals, by these things they are destroyed (Jude 9-10).

It was apostolic preaching which turned the world upside down and led to the fall of the Roman Empire that opposed the gospel. We must never forget that it is the truth that sets men free. There is no greater power in the heavens or the earth than the word of God, proclaimed in the power of the Holy Spirit.

This is our purpose, to be witnesses to the creation that the word of God is true, and more powerful than all of the powers of darkness, able even to redeem those who have fallen to the greatest depths. Let us always remember that: **"The Son of God appeared for this purpose, that He might destroy the works of the devil" (I John 3:8),** and we have been given that same purpose, as He stated in John 17:18: **"As Thou didst send Me into the world, I also have sent them into the world."** We have been sent into the world *for the same reason* that Jesus was sent into the world—to destroy the works of the devil. The weapons of our warfare were given to us for casting down enemy strongholds. It should be the resolve of every Christian to destroy the works of the devil, but we must do it in the strength and wisdom of the Lord. He was the light of this world and then He called the church the light of this world. Therefore, we must resolutely shine into the darkness.

The power of apostolic preaching is founded upon an apostolic lifestyle. This is a life that is utterly committed to doing all things for the sake of the gospel of Jesus Christ, to live the message as well as preach it, to build upon the only foundation with pillars of truth, and to give all that we have to Him who gave us all that He had.

**I urge you therefore, brethren, by the mercies of God, to present your bodies a living and holy sacrifice, acceptable to God, which is your spiritual service of worship.**

**And do not be conformed to this world, but be transformed *by the renewing of your mind*, that you may prove what the will of God is, that which is good and acceptable and perfect (Romans 12:1-2).**

**But you did not learn Christ in this way,**

**if indeed you have heard Him and have been taught in Him, just as truth is in Jesus,**

**that, in reference to your former manner of life, you lay aside the old self, which is being corrupted in accordance with the lusts of deceit,**

**and that you be *renewed in the spirit of your mind*,**

**and put on the new self, which in the likeness of God has been created in righteousness and holiness of the truth (Ephesians 4:20-24).** ■

**Rick Joyner** is the Executive Director of *MorningStar Publications* and Editor of *The Morning Star Journal* and *The Morning Star Prophetic Bulletin*. He is the author of numerous books, including **The Harvest, There Were Two Trees in the Garden, The World Aflame,** and his most recent release, **Epic Battles of the Last Days**. He is also the pastor of *MorningStar Fellowship* and the Director of the *MorningStar School of Ministry*. Rick and his wife Julie have three daughters, Anna, Aaryn and Amber, and two sons, Ben and Samuel. They live in Charlotte, NC.

# THE ULTIMATE TEST OF TRUE CHRISTIANITY

—— by ——

*John G. Lake*

*All Scriptures KJV unless otherwise indicated.*

The test of the Spirit, and the only test of the Spirit Jesus ever gave, is the ultimate and final test. He said, **"Ye shall know them by their fruits. Do men gather grapes of thorns, or figs of thistles?" (Matthew 7:16).**

If you want to test whether any present outpouring of the Spirit of God is the real, pure baptism of the Holy Ghost or not, test it by the fruits that it produces. If it is producing in the world, as we believe it is, a consciousness of God so high, so pure, so true, so like Christ, then it is the Holy Ghost Himself. No other test is of any value whatever.

The ultimate test to your own soul of the value of a thing that you have in your heart is the common test which Jesus gave, **"Ye shall know them by their fruits. Do men gather grapes of thorns, or figs of thistles?"**

Men tell us in these days that sin is what you think it is. Well, it is not. Sin is what God thinks it is. You might think according to your own conscience, but God thinks according to His. God thinks in accordance with the heavenly purity of His own nature. Man thinks in accordance with that degree of purity that his soul realizes. But the ultimate note is in God.

When men rise up in their souls' aspiration to the place of God's thought, then the character of Jesus Christ will be evident in their life; the sweetness of His nature, the holiness of His character, the beauty of the crowning glory that not only overshadowed Him, but that radiated from Him. The real life of the Christian is the inner life, the life of the soul. **"For out of the heart,"** said Jesus, **"proceed evil thoughts, murders, adulteries, fornications, thefts, false witness, blasphemies" (Matthew 15:19).** These are the things common to the flesh of man. Out of the soul of man, likewise, proceeds by the same law the beauty, virtue, peace, power and truth of Jesus, as the soul knows it.

He whose soul is joined to Christ may now, today, this hour, shed forth as a benediction upon the world the glory and blessing and peace and power of God, even as Jesus shed it forth to all men to the praise of God.

## The Earthly and Heavenly Materiality

One of most difficult things to make people understand is that the Spirit of God is a tangible substance; it is the essence of God's own being. We are composed of an earthly materiality; that is, our bodies are largely a composition of water and earth. This may sound a little crude, but the actual composition of a human being is about sixteen buckets of water and one bucket of earth. I am glad there is one bucketful of good mud in us! Water is a composition of gases, so you can see how much gas there is in mankind. But we are not all gas.

> ONE MUST BE THE RECIPIENT OF THE LIGHT, GLORY AND POWER OF GOD BEFORE HE CAN MANIFEST IT.

The composition of the personality of God—for God has a personality and a being and is a substance—is different from man's. Spirit is a substance. All heavenly things are of spiritual substance. The bodies of the angels are of some substance. They are not the same character of materiality as our own, for ours is an earthly materiality, but the composition of heavenly things is of a heavenly materiality. In other words, heavenly materiality is Spirit. The Word says, **"God is a Spirit: and they that worship him must worship him in spirit and in truth"** (John 4:24).

The spirit of a man must contact and know the real spirit of God. We do not know God with our flesh, with our hands or with our brains. We know God with our spirit. The knowledge of God that our spirit attains may be conveyed to us through the medium of our mind. The effect of God in our body comes through the medium of the spirit of man, through the mind of man into the body of man.

There is a quickening by the Spirit of God so that a man's body, a man's soul or mind, and a man's spirit become blessed, pervaded and filled with the presence of God Himself in us. The Word of God is wonderfully clear along these lines: **"Thou wilt keep him in perfect peace, whose mind is stayed on thee."** Why? **"Because he trusteth in thee"** (Isaiah 26:3). That is the peace that a Christian knows whose mind rests in God in perfect trust.

The Word of God says also that our flesh shall rejoice. Not our mind, but our very flesh shall rejoice. The presence of God is to be a living presence, not only in the spirit of man, nor in the mind of man alone, but also in the flesh of man, so that God is known in all the areas of his life. We know God in our very flesh; we know God in our mind; we know God in our spirit.

The medium by which God undertakes to bless the world is through the transmission of Himself. The Spirit of God is His own substance, the substance of His being, the very nature and quality of the presence and nature of God. Consequently, when we speak of the Spirit of God being transmitted to man, we are not talking about an influence, either spiritual or mental. We are talking about the transmission of the living substance and being of God into your being and into mine.

Not a mental effect, but a living substance, the living being and actual life transmitted, imparted, coming from God into your being.

That is the secret of the abundant life of which Jesus spoke. He said, **"I am come that they might have life, and that they might have it more abundantly"** **(John 10:10).** The reason we have the more abundant life is that, receiving God into our being, all the springs of our being are quickened by His living presence. Consequently, when we receive God we live life in a fuller measure. We live life with a greater energy because we become the recipients of the energy of the living God in addition to our normal energy, by receiving His being, His nature, His life into ours.

## The Radiating Glory of Transfiguration

The tremendous capacity of the human being to receive God is demonstrated by some of the incidents in the Word of God. The most remarkable in the Scriptures is the transfiguration of Jesus Himself, when the Spirit of God came upon Him so powerfully that it radiated from His being until His clothes became white and glistening, and His face shown as the light.

One must be the recipient of the light, glory and power of God before he can manifest it. Jesus demonstrated these two facts: the marvelous capacity of the nature of man to receive God into his being, and the marvelous capacity of the nature of man to reveal God. In the glory shining through His clothes, in the glistening of the glory of God upon His countenance, He demonstrated man's capacity to reveal God.

## The Spirit of God in Handkerchiefs and Cloths

The human being is the most marvelous and wonderful instrument of all the creation of God in its capacity to receive and reveal God. Paul received so much of God into his being that when men brought him their handkerchiefs and women brought him their aprons, and he took them into his hands, the handkerchiefs and aprons became impregnated with that living Spirit of God. When they were carried to one who was sick or possessed of devils, the Word says when they laid the handkerchiefs or aprons on them the Spirit of the living God passed from the handkerchief or apron into the sick, and the sick were healed and the devils were cast out.

People have been so in the habit of putting Jesus in a class by Himself that they have failed to recognize that He has made provision for the same living Spirit of God that dwelt in His own life, and of which He Himself was a living manifestation, to inhabit your being and mind, just as it inhabited the being of Jesus or Paul.

The story of the woman who touched the hem of Jesus' garment is a familiar one. Knowing how His whole being radiated that wondrous, blessed life of God, of which He Himself was the living manifestation, she said within herself, **"If I may but touch His garment" (Matthew 9:21),** and as she did so there flowed into her body the quickening life stream. She felt in her body that she was made whole of that plague. Conscious that something had flowed from Him, Jesus asked, **"Who touched my clothes?"**

His disciples replied, **"Thou seest the multitude thronging thee, and sayest** thou, Who touched me?" (Mark 5:31). But Jesus knew that someone had "touched" Him with a touch of faith, for **"virtue had gone out of him."** The Greek word used here for virtue means life, or the substance of His being—the quickening, living power of God, the very nature and being of God. If I transmit to another the virtue of my life, I simply transmit to another the life-power that is in me. The life of God that flows through me is transmitted to another. And so it was with Jesus.

The fact that people brought handkerchiefs and aprons to Paul, and they became impregnated with the Spirit of God and the people were healed when they touched them, is a demonstration in itself that any material substance can become impregnated with the same living Spirit of God.

## Divine Power in Gospel Papers

In my church in South Africa we published a paper in lots of ten thousand. We had the publishers send them to the tabernacle, and there we laid them out in packages of one or two hundred all around the front of the platform. At the evening service I would call certain ones of the congregation that I knew to be in contact with the living God to come and kneel and lay their hands on those packages of papers. Then we asked God that not only would the words in the paper be a blessing to those who received them, and that the message of Christ should come through the words printed on the paper, but we also asked God to make the very substance of the paper itself become filled with the Spirit of God. In the files in my tabernacle are thousands of letters from all parts of the world from people telling me that when they received our paper, the Spirit came upon them and they were healed. Or, when they received the paper, the joy of God came into their heart. Or they received the paper and were saved.

One woman wrote from South America, saying, "I received your paper. When I received it into my hands, my body began to vibrate so I could hardly sit on the chair, and I did not understand it. I laid the paper down, and after a while I took it up again; as soon as I had it in my hands I shook again. I laid it down and took it in my hands a third time; presently the Spirit of God came upon me so powerfully that I was baptized in the Holy Ghost."

This quality of the Spirit confuses the philosophers. It shows the clearest distinction which characterizes the real religion of Jesus Christ, and sets it apart from all other religions and all other ministries. The ministry of the Christian is the ministry of the Spirit. He not only ministers words to another, but he ministers the Spirit of God. It is the Spirit of God that inhabits the words, that speaks to the spirit of another and reveals Christ in and through him. ∎

---

*John G. Lake* had one of the most powerful ministries of modern times, establishing over 600 churches in Africa between 1908 and 1912. After returning to America due to the death of his wife, he established a healing ministry in Spokane, WA that resulted in over 100,000 verified healings in a 5 year period. Several biographies and books of his sermons have been written, inspiring multitudes of believers in our century. The above article was taken from a series of unpublished radio sermons.

# UNDERSTANDING OUR REAL PROBLEM

## by DeVern Fromke

TEACHING

**W**hat is your biggest problem—knowing the will of God, or doing the will of God? In the past 30 years I have asked this question dozens of times in meetings across the country. Some are quick to answer, and then wish they had not responded until later when they see just how revealing this question and their answer can be. There are some who insist, "If I really knew what God wanted, I would do it without a moment's hesitation. Why, I would pack up and leave for China tomorrow if I really knew that was God's will!" Yet others insist, "My problem is not knowing, but doing what I already know is God's will."

In Luke chapter six we have two incidents which reveal how the Pharisees thought they had a *head* problem—one of knowing—but Jesus showed them it was really a *heart* problem—one of doing. Consider this as we approach these incidents. Have you ever noticed how easy it is to allow the attitude of your heart to reach up and color the glasses of your mind? When you, for some reason, have an inner dislike for someone, it is so easy

to misinterpret what they do. An offended heart will latch on to an evil report of someone just like flypaper will attract a fly. And the proverbial phrase: "love is blind," is just as true in the opposite sense. When you really love or appreciate someone, it is quite difficult to misunderstand, or misinterpret their actions. Love has a way of understanding, of covering over mistakes and failures, of being blind to anything but the good.

It was a sabbath day and the Pharisees had observed how Jesus' disciples went through the fields, plucked ears of corn and did eat. Long before this, something had "crossed-up" these religious Pharisees. They had become critical and were nursing an offended spirit. Now, with colored glasses that desired only to accuse Jesus for allowing His disciples to break the sabbath traditions, they came announcing in effect, *"We have a head problem. We need to know why you do that which is not lawful on the sabbath days!"*

In Jesus' response there is a good rule to remember: you can never give a satisfactory answer to an offended heart; it wants to accuse—not understand. Answers will never work where unveilings are needed. So Jesus proceeded to show them how theirs was not really a *head* problem, but a *heart* problem. They had allowed their wicked, rebellious heart to confuse their mind—and color their viewpoint.

He started the unveiling by asking this question: *"Have you not read what David did when he went into the sanctuary where none but the priests could go? He took of the shewbread for himself and his men."* How pointed was His question! They could not miss the deepest implications. Jesus was simply saying: *"How is it that you sit in judgment on me and my disciples for plucking corn, yet you glory in King David and his men? In principle it is exactly the same."*

It was like saying: *"You have colored glasses. You do not misinterpret or even question what"* David had done because *you have not been crossed-up by him. You sing the praises of David and have become blind to his actions. But because your inner spirit has been offended by me, you misinterpret almost everything I or my disciples do."*

No more words were needed! There is something about the moral integrity of conscience that requires consistency. They well knew Jesus had unveiled that their real trouble was an offended heart which then affected their thinking. To make this plain, let us enlarge a little. Fenelon said, "Pure religion resides in the will alone." By this he meant that when the will, as the governing power in man's nature, is set right, all the rest of the nature must come into harmony. By the will I do not mean

## ANSWERS WILL NEVER WORK WHERE UNVEILINGS ARE NEEDED.

the wish of the man, or even his purpose, but rather the deliberate choice, the deciding power, the king—all that is in the man must yield obedience. Thus the mind will begin to lose its bias or colored glasses when the will is set for God.

When God is to take possession of us, it must be into this central will or personality that He enters. If, then, He is reigning there by the power of His Spirit, all the rest of our nature must come under His sway. As the will is, so is the man.

Finally, in answering the Pharisees, all Jesus needed to remind them was that the One who had made and designed the sabbath in the beginning surely should know how to use it properly. But is there some reader who still ponders why God did not strike David dead when he invaded this holy place reserved only for the Levites duly sanctified? The problem is simply this, that from our human viewpoint we can know only fragments. God must lift us into His own viewpoint if we would understand His fuller reasons.

You recall that David was a type of the Lord Jesus. Which means that if Jesus is our Prophet, Priest and King, then so was David, as a type, to fulfill that three-fold function. Since our Lord Jesus was a Priest after the higher order of Melchizedek, instead of the Aaronic order, He had the right to enter the Holy Place. For this same reason, God allowed His servant David, whom He considered after the Melchizedek order, this higher priesthood privilege. In man's limited viewpoint there are so many things we cannot understand.

But it is usually because we look only upon the lower order and do not see the eternal order of things. God has reasons and purposes which can never be known by the natural mind, and He will only share these as our heart opens to Him even as the flower opens to the sun.

Could these jealous, green-eyed Pharisees understand the actions of Jesus? No, they could not, for they *would not*. It was not a matter of the Holy Spirit being unwilling to unveil truth to them. While their conscience condemned them for their inconsistency, only repentance could rid them of their mental block.

Immediately in verse six, we are introduced to another incident which has an identical setting. Again it was a sabbath day and the same accusing crowd was there to find fault. One wonders why they didn't leave Him alone if they couldn't understand or appreciate His actions. The fact is this: no one can leave Him alone.

## GOD ONLY REQUIRES US TO WALK IN THE LIGHT WE HAVE, THAT IS, OBEY WHAT WE KNOW TO BE TRUTH NOW.

He is ever disturbing and crowding men to make a governmental choice. He never leaves anyone neutral. Every word spoken and every encounter with Him forces men to a decision of one kind or another. So should our preaching not only enlighten the mind, but also expose the heart.

When Jesus saw they were once again ready to accuse Him for His actions on the sabbath, He took the initiative. He did not wait for them, but precipitated an opportunity to once again reveal their *heart-trouble*.

He put the poor fellow with the withered hand on the spot by asking him to rise up and stand forth in their midst. This was a crucial moment for the poor man. Would he stay snuggled in the crowd where his withered condition would not show so obviously? In doing this, he would remain identified with the accusing crowd. But if he dared to move out and separate himself, it was like taking sides with Jesus against His accusers. What an inward rending there must have been before a governmental choice could be made. It meant either obedience or disobedience.

There is another interesting thing about this first command to the poor man. Jesus always asks of us something we *can do if we will*. Was there anything wrong with the man's legs? Could he stand up and walk forward? Of course he could! Did he understand clearly what action to take? Without doubt! This is always what we can expect as a principle in God's dealings.

But if the mind would take its directions from a heart that begins to rebel, it will go through something like this: The enemy will be there to divert the attention and "throw a curve," announcing: "You can't do what is asked." By confusing the issue, he will divert the mind from the immediate action to some distant impossibility. Thus the attention is focused upon some *other issue*, and the confused mind overlooks the immediate issue which the individual *can do if he will*! But we see, without confusion or distraction from the real issue, the man obeyed. He could use his legs, and he did. It meant a real exposure of his withered condition and a deliberate taking sides with the Lord Jesus. The cardinal issue is: if you will *do*—you shall *understand*.

I n every meeting there are those who hear our Lord insist that they rise up and stand forth, but the rebellious heart convinces the mind it will not be appropriate for a believer to allow some outward withered condition in his life to be exposed before the eyes of all the brethren. After all, it will ruin his testimony and weaken his influence among those he would like to help. What is forgotten is that others already sense that withered condition. We must understand that it is really an inward withered will which produces every outward withered condition.

Next, Jesus proceeded to unveil their hearts by asking this simple question: *"Is it lawful to do good on the sabbath day or evil?"* Of course they could not answer. If they acknowledged that it was permissible for Him to do good on the sabbath, they would be allowing Him to heal the withered arm. But they would rather maintain their consistency of tradition and doctrine than see a poor man healed. And there are many like them today, whose hardness of heart equals these Pharisees' indifference.

While they stood completely silent and dumbfounded by their inability to answer Him, Jesus turned to the man with the withered arm. The Pharisees' hearts had been exposed, and the real captivity of their mind unveiled. But the poor man with the withered arm had also been exposed. By his obedience to the Lord, he had received an inward work of healing. In yielding to the Lord Jesus, there came an infusion of His own life and strength within. The man had done what

he *could do* and now would receive the power to complete the next request: "Stretch forth thy hand."

The Lord now had an inner beachhead from which to work. And here is another rule we can always go by: once the inner government of our will is in perfect harmony with His will, He can move from this inner beachhead to fix up all the outward withered conditions in the life. Whether we have recognized it or not, God works from *inner to outward*. As long as man would seek to *use* Him for his own benefit, he is mostly concerned with the outward healing—that is, what God can do for him. What a difference when one is properly adjusted in the inner relationship and concerned only for what he can be unto God for Himself! Though we cannot see it working, the inner healing always prepares the way for the healing of all outward circumstances in the life. Was it not so with this poor man with the withered arm?

P erhaps the reader has imagined, "My withered hands just cannot hand out that tract; my withered legs buckle under me when I would stand for a testimony or stand alone for some issue I know is right; my withered lips tremble so I cannot praise Him as I know I ought to." Perish the thought! It is first the withered will which controls all these outward withered members.

One could hardly imagine how these Pharisees could be "filled with madness" even to the point of wanting to destroy Him! Yet any heart that is resisting God is blinded by its own foolish ways and will not follow intelligent reason. Such a deceitful heart has reasons the mind knows nothing about. It cannot rejoice and bless God—even for things that are good.

We are back to our first question: What is our biggest problem—*knowing* or *doing* the will of God? Like these Pharisees, many people have confused the issue until they do not *know*. But Jesus put it quite tersely in these words: "*If any man will do my will, he shall know of the doctrine . . .*"

There is a pathway of constant *knowing* and *doing*. These two, knowing and doing, like the two wings of a bird, are both necessary for any progress. There must be a constant cooperation between the mind and the will. God takes the first initiative in giving man what he needs to know. Then man is responsible for the choice of his will and God does the performing (doing). By this response man is then lifted to the next step where once again God shares what is needed for the next level of life. Man must once again respond. We can depend on this as a sure principle: God only requires us to walk in the light we have, that is, to obey what we know to be truth now.

Yet this is where man gets stalled. Did you ever sit at a checkerboard for several minutes waiting for the other player to move and you finally ask him, "It's your move, isn't it?" only to hear him reply, "No, it is your move!" I think this is what most folk do with God. After months and often years of "waiting for God to move," they suddenly discover that He has already made the last move. He has been waiting for their response to what He has already made known before they can be moved to the next step.

If they would only listen, He would remind them, "I've already shared what you need to know now. Just act on that." But too often the enemy has diverted their attention to some difficult issue ten years down the road when they could be joyfully using His resources for this immediate response.

When God is "working in us to will," we must set our faces like a flint to carry out this will, and must respond with an emphatic "I will" to every "thou shalt" of His. For God can only carry out His own will with us as we consent to it and *will* in harmony with Him. So the stairway of maturity is a continuous pathway of *knowing* and *doing*. ■

**DeVern Fromke** is the author of several books that would almost certainly be found on the list of great Christian works written during the last half of the 20th century, including **The Ultimate Intention** and **Unto Full Stature**. Because of DeVern's unyielding commitment to the centrality of Christ, he has not been blown about by the many winds of doctrine to sweep the church, and his teaching ministry continues to be a stabilizing influence in the church. This article is excerpted from **Unto Full Stature**, published by *Sure Foundations* and available through *MorningStar* or your local bookstore.

# TEACHING

## MOVING FROM MILK TO MEAT

by Steve Thompson

*All Scriptures KJV unless otherwise indicated.*

Over the past decade God has been restoring the church to our foundation of simplicity of devotion to Christ. Prior to this, many were wearied from attempting to fulfill our calling to "win the world for Christ" without understanding our privilege of relationship with Him. In large measure, God has corrected our vision and understanding so that intimacy with God is now understood as our primary purpose. However, in this process many have unwittingly rejected any calling beyond intimacy with God. Now the church is standing at a crossroads. If we do not take the next step that lies before us, we will stagnate and not fulfill our purpose. We must now begin working with the Lord in His harvest if we are to mature into the Bride that He has destined us to become.

## Jesus' Meat

Jesus is our model. He is our example. He obviously understood the calling to intimacy with His Father and walked in the fullness of it. When tempted by Satan in the wilderness, Jesus stated that man did not live by bread alone, but by every word that proceeds from the mouth of God. He was saying that He lived by the communication that was born of His intimacy with the Father. This was His bread. But later He spoke of the meat that He also possessed:

**In the mean while his disciples prayed him, saying, Master, eat.**

**But he said unto them, I have meat to eat that ye know not of.**

**Therefore said the disciples one to another, Hath any man brought him aught to eat?**

**Jesus saith unto them, My meat is to do the will of him that sent me, and to finish his work (John 4:31-34).**

Consider the circumstances surrounding Jesus' statement. He and His disciples had traveled quite a distance by foot. Jesus was weary from His journey and was waiting for His disciples, who had gone into the city to purchase food. While resting, even though He was fatigued, He began ministering to a Samaritan woman. When His disciples returned with the meat they had bought to strengthen Him, He made this statement to them. As was His custom, He was calling them to a higher truth than was apparent. Although He was weary from His journey, Jesus realized that His true nourishment came not from meat, but from doing His Father's will and accomplishing His work.

## An Anemic Church

Many believers today find themselves in a state of weariness. In fact, an accurate description of much of the church would be *anemic*. Anemia is characterized by listlessness and weakness. Physically, anemia can be caused by a failure to get enough iron in our food, often arising from a lack of meat in our diet. In the same way, many are spiritually anemic because they have not partaken of the meat that Jesus spoke of—*doing the will of the Father and finishing His work.*

Our failure to be engaged in doing the Father's will and work has indeed left much of the church weak and immature. In fact, many believers would mature more spiritually in six months by beginning to do the work of the ministry than they have in six years of simply receiving ministry. It is imperative that we recognize this truth—while we need to *hear God's voice* to live, we must *do His will* in order to grow and mature.

## Consumers or Producers

In the early days of our Christian experience, the excitement of God meeting our needs supernaturally consumed most of us. Just as a newborn receives all of his sustenance, both physically and emotionally, from nursing at his mother's breast, so we are fulfilled in receiving all that we need from God. The problem is that many enjoyed the comfort and security of the Father's breast too much to mature, and wanted to remain in that comfort zone. However, the time has come that we mature to the place where we desire to be not only a recipient, but a source of blessing to others.

This mind-set of passively receiving ministry has desperately weakened the church in Western society. Part of the problem arises because we dwell in the midst of a consumer-oriented culture and have allowed ourselves to be conformed to our world. In fact, it would be fair to say that the majority of our church members are simply looking for better teaching to help them grow spiritually. While it is true that understanding correct doctrine and receiving in-depth teaching are a part of God's methods to mature us spiritually, it is only a portion of His plan.

## Doing the Work

The first type of meat that Jesus outlined was *doing the Father's will*. God's will is revealed in His word. So being a hearer of the word is important. But, as James pointed out, if we are only hearers and not doers, then we are in self-deception (see James 1:22). However, when we become doers of the word, God's ways become engrafted into our souls. We begin to grow by receiving

His power in order to perform His word. No amount of teaching we receive can substitute for the growth that comes as we begin to obey the teaching we have already heard. This is primary to our maturity—*doing the will of His Father.*

Consider John's statement concerning Jesus in John 1:14:

**And the Word was made flesh, and dwelt among us, (and we beheld his glory, the glory as of the only begotten of the Father,) full of grace and truth.**

It is time that the word is made flesh in us as well. Just as Jesus contained the complete concept of all that God is in flesh, it is time that that which has been conceptual in our lives becomes a functioning part of us. Until the word of God becomes an integral part of our actions as well as our thoughts, so that it becomes our first nature, we will only be theoretical believers. We must go beyond theory to reality.

The world has seen and been repulsed by a church that professes grand concepts while contradicting those with our lives. Just as Jesus, by His life, drew the hurting and oppressed to the Father, so we will draw them as we begin to do that which we have believed. The word must become flesh in us.

The second thing that Jesus declared as being His meat was *finishing the work God had given Him to do.* Each of us is created for a purpose. Contrary to some popular teachings, Adam was not created solely to have intimacy with God. He was also created to accomplish a purpose and fulfill a mandate (see Genesis 1:26-28). Until we discover our purpose and begin to accomplish that which we were created for, we will remain immature at best.

# Becoming Teachers

Part of our purpose both individually and corporately is to disciple the nations and teach them to obey the Lord's commandments (see Matthew 28:18-20). In this light, consider the admonition by the writer of the book of Hebrews:

**For when for the time ye ought to be teachers, ye have need that one teach you again which be the first principles of the oracles of God; and *are become such as have need of milk, and not of strong meat.***

**For every one that useth milk is unskilful [has no experience] in the word of righteousness: for he is a babe.**

**But strong meat belongeth to them that are of full age, even those who by reason of use have their senses exercised to discern both good and evil.**

**Therefore leaving the principles of the doctrine of Christ, let us go on unto perfection [maturity] (Hebrews 5:12-6:1, margin notes in brackets).**

Although written in the first century, this passage is as applicable in the twentieth century as it was then. The time had arrived that these believers should be doing the teaching, not just receiving it. However, because they had not experienced the growth that comes through *doing the work*, they still needed someone to nurse them in the basics. Our growth is stunted when we only receive teaching; we must begin to mature through exercising our gifts as we train and equip others.

As an illustration, a friend who was a commercial pilot once told me that he had reached a plateau in his skills as an aviator at a certain point in his career. No amount of further teaching or training would help him mature beyond where he was. It was not until he became a flight instructor that he broke from this plateau and resumed growing professionally as a pilot. As he began training others, he matured into his full potential.

Most believers today have more knowledge about the Bible than the first century disciples, and possibly more than the first century apostles. In fact, the New Testament was just being written by the apostles during the first century. Yet they were able to turn their world upside down, because they were busy doing the ministry, not just studying about it.

## We Gather, God Scatters

Our basic strategy in the West has been to gather all of the best saints together in one location in order to build a dynamic church. Upon examination, God's plan may be somewhat different. When the church was birthed at Jerusalem, almost immediately they became communal and were quite happy meeting together and enjoying the presence of the Lord. This was a joyous season for the early believers, and it was a necessary time in their development. However, it did not last, nor was it supposed to. God soon chose to scatter them abroad from Jerusalem in order to plant them, so that they could mature as He had desired. They could only continue growing as they began bearing fruit.

Today God is preparing to scatter many in the church abroad as seeds that they might grow into the trees of righteousness they are called to be. Many pastors and leaders are beginning to catch a vision of something larger than their own congregations; they are beginning to see the kingdom of God and His

---

✳ *Mustard Seeds of Wisdom*

*Every age has its own characteristics. Right now we are in an age of religious complexity. The simplicity which is in Christ is rarely found among us. In its stead are programs, methods, organizations and a world of nervous activities which occupy time and attention.*

— A. W. TOZER

purposes. Some are sowing their best people into barren fields in order that they might mature and bear fruit. Many believers are looking for a fulfillment in their souls that only comes through entering the labor of the Lord.

## Spiritual Socialism

Another factor that has hindered the church's ability to produce mature saints is the cultural/political force of socialism. Socialism is the socio-political ideology of centralizing all modes of business and government in a society. While managing to increase efficiency initially, this social system eventually destroys the pillars of personal responsibility and individual initiative in society, thereby weakening that society as a whole. At this point, the society will logically deteriorate into communism and the accompanying decay unless there is a revolutionary intervention reinstating individual rights and personal responsibility.

Socialism is demonic in its origin, and the enemy's strategic purpose in it is to destroy leadership before it develops. Socialism removes the need for individual leadership by centralizing all decision-making and investing it in a small number of elite administrators. This effectively stifles initiative, innovation and achievement—all of which are characteristics of maturity. When individuals are given responsibility, they will almost invariably grow through having to creatively fulfill that responsibility. Unless individuals are trained and allowed to function as a vital part of society they will never contribute, but instead function as passive members in that society.

Consider much of the church today. We have created a system where people can simply show up to a few meetings, pay their tithes (at least occasionally) and then think that they are doing God's will. We both require and expect little from them and they return it in full. Many who could be powerfully used of the Lord never will be, because they are seldom challenged to stand with the Lord on their own at the appropriate time. Consider Jesus' plan to train leaders and to release them into ministry. We find His plan in Matthew 11:28-29:

**Come unto me, all ye that labour and are heavy laden, and I will give you rest.**

**Take my yoke upon you, and learn of me; for I am meek and lowly in heart: and ye shall find rest unto your souls.**

When we come to the Lord initially He gives us rest. But this is not the end of the matter. There still remains a rest for those who come to Him. If we will take the next step and take His yoke upon us, in other words, become engaged in working with Him, we will then find rest unto our souls. Rest in our souls and inner peace are signs of maturity, but they will only be birthed in us as we begin to labor with the Lord in ministry, taking increased responsibility for ourselves and those we minister to.

The spiritual socialism in the church has been devastating to our people. We have allowed our people to be robbed of the blessing of having creativity and initiative released in them by providing for them what they need to find for themselves. Many have not learned to pray and seek God for themselves because both they and the leaders have been content to have others pray for them. In many streams of the church, some leaders have been willing to do all of the ministry instead of training the church to do it. We may think this is noble, and even self-sacrificing on our part, but we have not only sacrificed ourselves, but the maturity of those we should be training to handle ministry situations.

Many leaders attempt to protect those in their charge by handling all of the tough assignments. If we do not start training our people to heal the sick, deal with demons, and love those who are unlovable, then we are simply overprotective parents who will never allow their "children" to grow through experiencing life. In "protecting" our church members from shouldering the responsibility of ministry, we have stolen from them what they desperately need to grow and mature—*the meat of doing His work.*

## The Heart or the Hands

In 1987, the Lord appeared to me in a dream and asked me the following question, "What is the difference between a loving wife and a harlot, the heart or the hands?" Not understanding that the Lord never asks us a question because He needs an answer, I foolishly told Him, "the heart." He simply said, "Look at Proverbs 31," and the dream ended.

Upon waking I quickly turned in my Bible to the 31st proverb and began discovering my error. This proverb has six different references to the hands of a virtuous wife serving her husband. As I studied and prayed over this matter, I determined that even the heart of a harlot is with a man as long as he is in her presence. The difference in a wife is that her hands serve her husband while he is away from her. If my wife loves me she will not only desire intimate communication with me while I am home, but she will also want to serve and "take care of business" while I am away.

Though we may love to sit with the Lord when He is present, we must also love Him enough to serve Him with our hands in His absence, or we are no better than a harlot. If we are to be His virtuous wife, then we must learn this lesson: worship may begin with intimate fellowship in His presence, but it also encompasses hard work, including taking care of His children.

## The Miracle of Marriage

A wise man once said that the miracle of marriage and parenting was not that adults produce children, but *that children produce adults.* Indeed, raising children produces a maturity within the parents that could not be accomplished through other means. It is not until we have responsibility for others that we ourselves are forced to mature in our faith and decision-making ability. It is also said that until one has children of their own, they will never really understand God's love. While I believe the essence of that statement I would broaden it to include having spiritual children as well. Until we produce and parent either natural or spiritual children, we will not fully mature in understanding God or manifesting His nature. The essence of spiritual maturity is becoming self-less and giving ourselves for others. Parent-hood and true ministry are the greatest vehicles for that, because both require serving God and others, not our-*selves*.

Selfishness is our greatest hindrance to maturity in God. Our focus on self keeps us in bondage and the only deliv-erance is to learn to love God and others. Like Jesus, we can have no greater love than that we lay down our lives for our friends. As we learn to lay down our lives for those we have birthed, selfish-ness is progressively removed from our lives, and we learn the joy of giving our lives for the good of others.

## Going On to Maturity

The weariness that many in the church are experiencing is not the result of an attack by the enemy. It is a message from God. He is urging you to move out in your calling, risk your reputation and give Him an opportunity to prove His faithfulness. The growth you have been seeking through receiving more teaching will begin to come as you step out to teach others. You will only find your strength and your maturity in God as you begin doing His will and finishing the work He has given to you.

Our life consists of much more than simply receiving teaching, it involves participating in the building of God's House and His Kingdom. It is time for those who have followed the Lord and have seen His works to be sent by Him to do His works. We cannot please the Father by going backwards or by con-tinuing in the state we presently are; we must go forward. As we do, we will find a power and maturity that we many have sought for years.

This year especially, God is extending a call to anyone who will hear His voice. Now is the time for His disciples to become His apostles. We, like the chil-dren of Israel, have left Egypt. We are now standing at the Jordan river of our generation. God is calling us to mature from simply being children that He cares for, to being warriors who will take the Promised Land. ■

## About The Author

**Steve Thompson** is the Vice President of *MorningStar Publications* and pastor of *Hartsville Community Fellowship*. He also trav-els throughout the U.S. teaching and minis-tering prophetically, while serving on the *MorningStar Ministry Team*. He and his wife Angie have two sons, Jon and Joshua. They reside in Charlotte.

# OUR PRIESTLY MINISTRY

— by —

## *Rick Joyner*

*All Scriptures NAS unless otherwise indicated.*

One of the great truths that was recovered and highlighted by the Reformation is the priesthood of all believers. This is a doctrine that almost all Protestants and Evangelicals believe. However, that which is so generally believed is often generally overlooked, and seldom implemented. This has been the case with the great truth about our priestly ministry.

What does it really mean to be a priest of the Most High God? This subject is so profound and expansive that it is not possible to fully answer it in a single article, but it is important that we review the fundamentals of this crucial matter. There are few things that we can do to so change our lives, the church, and the world in general, as beginning to live this truth.

## The Foundation of All Ministry

What is a priest? This term was generally understood by both the Jews and pagans during the first century. The early Christians derived their understanding from the Old Covenant type, which was still active in the temple in Jerusalem. But the modern evangelical church does not have this advantage. In general, little attention has been given to understanding this ministry that is supposed to be a basic function for New Covenant believers.

When the institutional church tried to implement these truths, it did what is natural for an institution to do; it institutionalized them. This actually separated these truths from the lives of all but a few professionals. The Reformation quickly recovered the truth that this is a ministry all believers are called to, but the recovery of the practical application of this truth has still made little progress in the actual life of the church. Where progress has been made, its effect has been profound. This truth is a major part of the foundation of all ministry, and to the degree that it is neglected, our foundation has been weakened.

Under the Old Covenant, the priest was the primary spiritual mediator between God and men. He was not the only mediator, because the Lord raised up prophets as spokesmen, and He was represented in civil matters by the kings and elders. The priests were commissioned to mediate for the people in the area of relationship with the Lord, and the civil authority was commissioned to mediate for the people in their civil relations with each other.

Because the function of the Old Covenant priest was to a great degree devoted to the offering of the sacrifices and performing the rituals required by the Law, it is easy to understand how the institutional church would succumb to such a high degree of ritual in the development of her priestly offices. It is also easy to understand how these functions would be delegated to a special class of professionals. The Old Covenant type was a single tribe of the Israelites, the Levites, who were designated specifically for this function, with a very strict ban on allowing anyone from the other tribes to perform these duties. However, to understand the types properly, we must first understand that with the change of covenants the Lord profoundly changed the rules by which men are now allowed to approach Him.

**For there is one God, and one mediator also between God and men, the man Christ Jesus (I Timothy 2:5).**

Jesus is now the only mediator between God and men. We partake of this ministry only as we abide in Him. Our goal for this ministry is to introduce others to Him, and to help them to so connect to Him that they no longer need us. Even so, this is not our main function as priests. *Our main function is to minister to the Lord.*

**Now when these things have been thus prepared, the priests are continually entering the outer tabernacle, performing the divine worship (Hebrews 9:6).**

The ministry in the Outer Court was to the people, but the ministry in the tabernacle was to the Lord. Here we see that the priests were **"continually entering"** the tabernacle to perform this divine worship, or ministry, to Him. Much of what we consider ministry, what we usually devote most of our time to in ministering, is the Outer Court ministry to the people. This is the reverse of what we should be doing in ministry.

## The Foundation of the Priestly Ministry

The first responsibility of all in ministry is to minister to the Lord, not men. The ministry that we have to men should be the result of our ministry to the Lord. All true spiritual fruit will come as the result of our union with Him. When we give ourselves to the Lord first, we will have much more to give to the people. The anointing comes from the presence of the Lord. We can have the best teachings ever articulated, but have no true spiritual fruit if the Holy Spirit does not endorse it with His anointing.

**And as for you, the anointing which you received from Him abides in you, and you have no need for anyone to teach you; but as His anointing teaches you about all things, and is true and is not a lie, and just as it has taught you, you abide in Him (I John 2:27).**

This is not saying that we do not need teachers, for they were given by the Lord to the church for the equipping of His people. However, teaching without the anointing does not profit us spiritually. The purpose of all ministry is to draw us closer to the Lord, that we may more fully abide in Him; He does not anoint teaching or preaching that does not originate from Him and draw men to Him.

For example, we can teach our people about unity so that they understand every aspect of the doctrine, but that does not necessarily unify them. Let the right circumstances come along, and there will be a great division if the knowledge that they have in their minds has not been transferred to their hearts. **"For with the *heart* [not the mind] man believes, resulting in righteousness" (Romans 10:10).** Knowledge without the anointing may stimulate our minds, and we may intellectually agree with it, but we will only live it if it has been transferred to our hearts by the Holy Spirit. We get the anointing from being in the presence of the Lord.

Upon entering the first compartment of the tabernacle, there was a golden lampstand on the left which burned olive oil for light, representing the Holy Spirit. There was the table of shewbread on the right, and at the far end, the altar of incense. The table of shewbread had twelve loaves of bread on it, symbolizing the twelve tribes of Israel. They were set in two rows to symbolize their unity (in Scripture the number two often symbolizes unity, i.e., "the two shall become one" [see Genesis 2:24]). As a part of the service in the tabernacle, wine was poured as an oblation in front of the table. This made the table a prophecy of communion, or the common union, of God's people in Christ. The reason that the loaves were in unity, representing this communion, was because it was directly across from the lampstand, continually bathed in the light of the Holy Spirit, or the anointing. As the apostle John so wonderfully stated it:

**If we walk in the light as He Himself is in the light, we have fellowship [Greek *koinonea*, "communion"] with one another, and the blood of Jesus His Son cleanses us from all sin (I John 1:7).**

True unity comes from abiding in the light with the Son of God together. Anything less will be superficial at best. Those who abide in the light will not be prone to do things that create division. Our job as priests is not to just go out to tell the people about the light in the Holy Place, but to lead the people into that light. In Christ, *all* are called to be priests, and *all* must learn to "continually enter" His presence to perform this divine service. Those who do not learn to abide in that place will not remain unified, regardless of how much we talk about it.

**But *we all*, with unveiled face beholding as in a mirror the glory of the Lord, are being transformed into the same image from glory to glory, just as from the Lord, the Spirit (II Corinthians 3:18).**

Teaching is important, but people are not changed just by knowing the doctrines—they must behold the glory of the

Lord. A few minutes in the manifest presence of the Lord can accomplish more than many weeks, or even years, of teaching. Teaching that comes from the presence of the Lord, which is anointed by the Holy Spirit, will lead those who hear into His presence, where the knowledge is transferred from the mind to the heart.

# The Altar of Incense

The altar of incense, also located in the Holy Place, represents prayer and intercession. David wrote, **"May my prayer be counted as incense before Thee; the lifting up of my hands as the evening offering" (Psalm 141:2; see also Revelation 8:4).** The Lord said that His house was to be **"a house of prayer for all nations" (Luke 19:46 NIV).** This implies that one of the main purposes of the house that He has chosen to dwell in is for prayer for all people. Never did He say that His house would be a house of preaching, a house of healing, or even a house of fellowship. Certainly all of these are found in His house, but He obviously meant for prayer to be foremost. Therefore, if we are to be His dwelling place, prayer should be our highest priority.

One way that we are able to dwell continually in the presence of the Lord to perform the divine service was explained when the building of the altar of incense was first commissioned.

> **And Aaron shall burn fragrant incense on it; he shall burn it every morning when he trims the lamps.**
>
> **And when Aaron trims the lamps at twilight, he shall burn incense. There shall be perpetual incense before the Lord throughout your generations (Exodus 30:7-8).**

Aaron was to light the incense as his first duty each morning and as the last thing he did at night, but there would also be, **"perpetual incense before the Lord."** This statement implies that if we will learn to begin our days with prayer, and then end them in prayer, we will be able to stay in a perpetual attitude of prayer, being aware of His presence continually. The Lord does not just want us to talk to Him a couple of times a day, He wants us to abide in Him—continually.

If we really are His temple, and His Spirit abides in us, how is it that we ignore Him so much? The Lord wants to have fellowship with us in all that we do. How much would our typical day change if the Lord appeared in the flesh first thing in the morning, and went with us everywhere each day? The truth is, that if the eyes of our hearts were opened, we would see Him in everything that we do, and the reality of His presence would actually be greater than that which we are seeing with our physical eyes. Then we would also manifest the sweet aroma of the knowledge of Him in every setting and circumstance, as we are called to do as His dwelling place.

As Paul explained,

> **Now these things [the experiences of Israel in the wilderness] happened to them as an example, and they were written for our instruction, upon whom the ends of the ages have come (I Corinthians 10:11).**

The Lord does not want literal incense rising to Him, as he explained later through the prophets, but He does want our prayers. Instead of "thinking to ourselves," He wants us to be conversing with Him.

**We are destroying speculations and every lofty thing raised up against the knowledge of God, and we are taking every thought captive to the obedience of Christ (II Corinthians 10:5).**

We will find that if we take the time to properly light this fire the first thing in the morning, and then as the last thing we do at night, soon there will be a perpetual prayer as incense before the Lord rising from our hearts.

## The Place of Sacrifice

The priesthood is, from beginning to end, a place of sacrifice. When people first entered the Outer Court, the first thing they saw was the altar of burnt offering where the sacrifices were made. The priests who served there were usually covered in blood and guts. It was not a pretty sight, just as the cross was not the pretty stained-glass window scene we have tried to make it out to be. Death on the cross was one of the most perverted and cruel exhibitions of the demented human mind. But the Lord is not just trying to change us—He's trying to kill us! True Christianity requires the ultimate price—the "whole burnt offering," which means our whole life must be placed on the altar.

The fire on the altar of incense was originally lit from the fire on the altar of burnt offerings, which typified the cross. It does require sacrifice to pray. We must give up our self-life. The Lord is not just after a few minutes of our day—He wants every thought to be taken captive and made obedient to Him. Modern Western Christianity is a far cry from the Christianity found throughout the rest of the world, or its biblical counterpart. More than any other place or time, Western Christianity is in the stranglehold of the Laodicean spirit of lukewarmness. If we are going to fulfill our calling for these times, we must embrace the reality of that which we have been proclaiming for the last five hundred years—we must all begin to walk in our calling to the priestly ministry. It is a difficult place, and it will require sacrifice, but this is the purpose for which we were apprehended by the Lord, and we must now answer the call.

**For the love of Christ controls us, having concluded this, that one died for all, therefore all died;**

**and He died for all, that they who live should no longer live for themselves, but for Him, who died and rose again on their behalf (II Corinthians 5:14-15).**

We are called to give Him "the sacrifice of praise," etc. There is a reason why the altar of incense is called an "altar"; it is a place of sacrifice. It requires sacrifice to perform our duties properly in ministry to the people. Our ministry as priests is founded upon sacrifice, and our effectiveness will be determined by the degree of our sacrifice, as we see in the following texts:

**For just as the sufferings of Christ are ours in abundance, so**

also our comfort is abundant through Christ.

But if we are afflicted, it is for your comfort and salvation; or if we are comforted, it is for your comfort, which is effective in the patient enduring of the same sufferings which we also suffer;

and our hope for you is firmly grounded, knowing that as you are sharers of our sufferings, so also you are *sharers* of our comfort.

For we do not want you to be unaware, brethren, of our affliction which came *to us* in Asia, that we were burdened excessively, beyond our strength, so that we despaired even of life;

indeed, we had the sentence of death within ourselves in order that we should not trust in ourselves, but in God who raises the dead (II Corinthians 1:5-9).

But we have this treasure in earthen vessels, that the surpassing greatness of the power may be of God and not from ourselves;

*we are* afflicted in every way, but not crushed; perplexed, but not despairing;

persecuted, but not forsaken; struck down, but not destroyed;

always carrying about in the body the dying of Jesus, that the life of Jesus also may be manifested in our body.

For we who live are constantly being delivered over to death for Jesus' sake, that the life of Jesus also may be manifested in our mortal flesh (II Corinthians 4:7-11).

For the love of Christ controls us, having concluded this, that one died for all, therefore all died;

and He died for all, that they who live should no longer live for themselves, but for Him who died and rose again on their behalf (II Corinthians 5:14-15).

For to you it has been granted for Christ's sake, not only to believe in Him, but also to suffer for His sake (Philippians 1:29).

and if children, heirs also, heirs of God and fellow heirs with Christ, if indeed we suffer *with Him* in order that we may also be glorified *with Him* (Romans 8:17).

Therefore, since Christ has suffered in the flesh, arm yourselves also with the same purpose, because he who has suffered in the flesh has ceased from sin (I Peter 4:1).

The apostle Paul is one of the great examples of the New Covenant ministry. He died daily. He did all things for the sake of the gospel. He sacrificed his own will, safety and comfort to serve the Lord and his people. Paul's great effectiveness in ministry can be directly tied to the degree to which he laid down his life for the purposes of the Lord.

There is power in sacrifice. The cross was the ultimate sacrifice, and it is the ultimate power. The degree to which we take up the cross daily will be the degree

THE MORNING STAR  35

to which we experience the power of God in our daily life. The priesthood is for intercession. Intercession is not prayer for yourself, but for others. The priesthood to which we are called is to live not for ourselves, but for others.

The ministry of intercession is the foundation of all ministry. Ministry is not living for ourselves but for others. Intercession is not just praying for ourselves but for others. The church is itself called to be a prophetic voice to the world, and we see this relationship between the prophetic ministry and intercession in Isaiah 62:6-7:

> **On your walls, O Jerusalem, I have appointed watchmen; all day and all night they will never keep silent. You who remind the LORD, take no rest for your-selves;**
>
> **And give Him no rest until He establishes and makes Jerusalem a praise in the earth (Isaiah 62:6-7).**

In I Samuel 12:23, Samuel declared: **"Moreover, as for me, far be it from me that I should sin against the LORD by ceasing to pray for you."** It would have been a sin against the Lord for the prophet to stop praying for the people, even though the people had just rejected the Lord by seeking a king for them-selves. It is true that, **"Where your treasure is, there will your heart be also" (Matthew 6:21).** If we have an investment of prayer and intercession in people's lives, we are much more likely to have a right heart toward them as well, and be able to represent the Lord to them without bias.

True spiritual authority is founded upon love. Jesus felt compassion for the sheep, so He became their Shep-herd—His ministry as Shepherd was founded upon His compassion. Jesus felt compassion for the people who lived in darkness, so He became their Teacher—His teaching ministry was founded upon His compassion. The same is true with us. We will not have true spiritual authority over any group, city, or nation that we do not love. This love will either be the fruit of intercession, or it will result in intercession, but either way it will be tied to intercession. If we love someone we will pray for them. If we don't love them, but start to invest in them through prayer, we will begin to love them, and the Lord can give us a true ministry for them.

✻ *Mustard Seeds of Wisdom*

*Almost every heresy is the result of men trying to carry to logical conclusions that which God has only revealed in part.*

*— Paul Cain*

Like everyone in ministry, I have been falsely accused, slandered, rejected and betrayed. I confess that this has often caused me to want to call fire down from heaven on those people, but the Lord commanded me to pray *for* them, not *against* them. At first, even praying for them every day, it took me several years to start to really feel love for some of them. Now I feel a great love for some of them. Then the Lord showed me that He was going to send me back to some of these groups and people, that they would become some of my best and most loyal friends, and that some of the greatest spiritual fruit was going to come from serving them. Had my first desires been realized, having these groups disbanded or worse, I would have missed an important part of my own ultimate destiny.

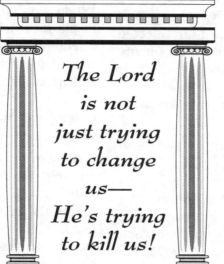

*The Lord is not just trying to change us—He's trying to kill us!*

Jesus, our High Priest, died for the very ones who cried, "Crucify Him!" So must we. He did not come to condemn the world; it was already condemned. Jesus came to save the world, and we have been sent to proclaim that great mercy of God. This mercy is most powerfully proclaimed when it is persecuted.

When we start to intercede for someone we make an investment in their life. This investment becomes a treasure, and where our treasure is, there will our heart also be—we start to love them. When we start to love someone we can become a vessel of spiritual authority that can speak prophetically into their life. This is how intercession becomes the foundation of prophetic ministry, which is what Samuel understood.

I usually know that when the Lord starts putting a country on my heart He is about to send me there. It is only after I have love for a country that He starts to speak to me about it. Even if the Lord gives me words of impending judgment for a country, I must love that country before I can deliver the words. Anything but divine love will pervert such messages. That is why He made Jeremiah love Israel so much that he would weep over her, even as he was foretelling her destruction.

Moses was denied the blessing of leading the people into their Promised Land because the Lord told him to speak to the rock to bring forth water, but he struck the rock in anger instead. As a prophet of the Lord, he represented the Lord as being angry when He was not, and it cost him dearly. Many prophetic people have disqualified themselves from higher realms of authority by representing the Lord improperly in this way. One of the devastating traps of the prophetic is for us to think that, because the Lord uses us occasionally to speak through, He is just like we are, and that our feelings are His feelings. This is why we must always be careful to distinguish our own feelings from that which is coming by the anointing.

"God is love," and we will only see as He sees when we love those we are beholding. Anything but love will distort our vision. I never trust "revelations" that come to me about those that I may have been personally rejected by when I still feel the wounds. Whenever I am rejected or attacked by someone they go on my prayer list. I pray for them and their ministry until I have such an investment in them that I love them and care what happens to them.

If bitterness gets a root in us it will defile ourselves and many more. Whenever someone tells me they have a word of correction or judgment for another person, ministry, etc., I always ask them if they love that person or ministry, and how much time they spent in prayer for them.

**Therefore He is also able to save to the uttermost those who come to God through Him, since He always lives to make intercession for them (Hebrews 7:25 NKJV).**

When Jesus saw what was wrong with the world, He did not condemn it, He laid down His life for it. All who have a true ministry will do the same. Jesus died for the very ones who rejected Him. We, too, can be given authority to help save those who reject us if we will intercede for them, as He exemplified: **"He is also able to save to the uttermost . . .** *since* **He always lives to make intercession for them."**

Just as the Lord had to be rejected and persecuted by the ones He came to save before He could save them, the same is often true of those in ministry. When we handle rejection properly, it can open a wide door for effective ministry. We **"overcome evil with good" (Romans 12:21).** We cannot overcome the evil until we have had a confrontation with it. When we maintain the fruit of the Spirit in the face of evil, we open the door for effective ministry. This is one reason why Paul suffered so much persecution, and he counted it as so valuable—persecution opens the door for ministry. That is why we must remain faithful to love our enemies.

However, just as the priesthood required ministry to the Lord first, we must always guard ourselves against loving the people more than we love the Lord. That will pervert the ministry by leading to unsanctified mercy, which is giving mercy to the things which God has under judgment. The only way that we can keep the proper balance of loving the people, but representing the Lord first to the people, is by loving Him more than we love them—but we must always love them. We must keep the first two great commandments in the order they were given.

Elijah prayed for the judgments of the Lord to come on the people, but it was not out of his own wrath. God's wrath is not like man's wrath. Neither is His jealousy like man's, which is self-centered. We must always be careful not to represent our anger as being the Lord's, or we can end up like Moses and never enter the fullness to which we have been called. ■

# READY FOR BATTLE

### by

## Kenneth Copeland

*All Scriptures KJV unless otherwise indicated.*

I have a question for you. It's one of the most serious questions you'll ever face. Your answer will profoundly affect not only your own life, but also the lives of countless others in the short time we have left before the return of Jesus. The question is this: Where will you be when God's glory sweeps the earth?

Will you be right in the midst of it, laying hands on the sick, preaching the gospel, working miracles by the power of God? Or will you be sitting in your living room with your feet up, watching television and missing out on the grandest moment this earth has ever known?

If you haven't already thought about it, I suggest strongly you do so right now, because you don't have much time to decide. There is a flood of glory coming. The first waves of it have already begun, and those who want to be a part of it need to get prepared—immediately!

This spiritual flood began nearly 2,000 years ago, on the Day of Pentecost, when the city of Jerusalem was shaken by a group of 120 believers who had just been baptized with the fire of the Holy Spirit. As thousands gathered to hear the gospel for the first time, each person hearing it spoken in his own language, Peter explained to them what was happening, saying:

**This is that which was spoken by the prophet Joel;**

**And it shall come to pass in the last days, saith God, I will pour out of my Spirit upon all flesh: and your sons and your daughters shall prophesy, and your young men shall see visions, and your old men shall dream dreams:**

**And on my servants and on my handmaidens I will pour out in those days of my Spirit; and they shall prophesy:**

**And I will show wonders in heaven above, and signs in the earth beneath; blood, and fire, and vapour of smoke:**

**The sun shall be turned into darkness, and the moon into**

blood, before that great and notable day of the Lord come:

And it shall come to pass, that whosoever shall call on the name of the Lord shall be saved (Acts 2:16-21).

Some people have assumed since Peter said, **"This is that which was spoken by the prophet Joel,"** that this whole prophecy has been fulfilled. But it hasn't. It has only been fulfilled in part.

As the *Amplified Bible* says, that was **"[the beginning of] what was spoken through the prophet Joel."** The fullness of the prophecy has yet to come. In fact, even as I write these words, the Holy Spirit is in the process of leading each one of us into the place we need to be so that these words spoken by Joel finally can be grandly and gloriously fulfilled.

Why is it so important that each one of us be in our place? Read those verses from Acts again and you'll see. In them, God tells us that when His servants and handmaidens prophesy, He will show wonders in heaven above, and signs in the earth beneath. Obviously, the servants and handmaidens have a special role in this outpouring of the Spirit. They must be doing what they're called to do. They must be anointed of God to stand in their appointed place of ministry while God is pouring His Spirit upon all flesh. That was true on the Day of Pentecost and it is still true today.

On that day, when the latter day rain of the Spirit began, about 120 of God's servants and handmaidens were gathered in the upper room, continuing in one accord in prayer and supplication (see Acts 1:14-15). They were in place, ready to move into the streets as soon as God's Spirit was poured out upon them. They were doing exactly what Jesus had told them to do.

The shameful part of it was, only about a third of those who had been instructed to be there were present. Jesus had appeared to more than 500 of them and told them all the same thing: **"tarry ye in the city of Jerusalem, until ye be endued with power from on high"** (Luke 24:49). Apparently, 380 of them decided to stay home and "watch TV instead."

## Beyond the Requirements

What's the difference between the 380 who didn't follow Jesus' instructions and the 120 who did? Those in the first group were merely Christians, those in the second group were God's servants and handmaidens.

The word translated servants and handmaidens in Acts 2:18 is the Greek word *doulos*. It is the same word used twice, once in the feminine form and once in the masculine form. In this particular instance, *doulos* refers to someone who has voluntarily subjected himself to another person's will. It describes a bondslave who could be free if he wanted to be, but chooses instead to be wholly subservient to another because of his love for that person.

It carries the idea of chivalry, or of a knight of the court who has authority and honor in his own right, yet because of his love for his king, he has pledged himself to that king, and to die for him if necessary. He has said, "Even though I have great rank and power, I bow my legions to you, my King. I'll be your champion. I'll fight your fights. I'll go in your name." If you are a servant or hand-maiden, that is the commitment you will make to your King, Jesus. It is not a commitment He forces upon you. It is one you make by choice.

You see, when you were born again, you did not become a servant of God. You became a child of God, a son or daughter of the Almighty. You were made free, and, **"if the Son therefore shall make you free, ye shall be free indeed" (John 8:36).** But if you truly love the One Who set you free, you will trade that freedom for a life of service to Him. That's what the apostle Paul did, for in Romans 1:1 he called himself **"a bond servant of Jesus Christ"** (AMP).

More than perhaps any other man, Paul knew what it was to be free. He was born a free Roman citizen. Then he was born again and received the revelation from God that he had been made free from the authority of darkness, and translated into the kingdom of God's dear Son. Yet he bowed his knee to Jesus and said, "I give away my freedom. I give away my will. I give it all away to serve You. I'll live for You and I'll die for You."

As Jesus Himself set the pattern for such servanthood during His earthly ministry, we are exhorted to follow His example:

**Let this mind be in you, which was also in Christ Jesus:**
**Who, being in the form of God, thought it not robbery to be equal with God:**

**But made himself of no repu-tation, and took upon him the form of a servant (Philippians 2:5-7).**

As a servant or handmaiden, your attitude will be like Jesus' attitude, **"Not my will, but thine, be done" (Luke 22:42).** You'll say, "I don't care what it takes, I will obey God. If He wants me to lock myself up in my closet and pray for eight hours every day, that's what I'll do because I'm His champion. I'm His bondslave!"

Some people like to argue that God would never require such sacrifices from us. That's just proof that those people aren't servants or handmaidens, because servants and handmaidens aren't inter-ested in doing only what God requires. They want to go beyond that. They want to be totally committed to God and His Word. They want everything they do to be governed by Him. As a result, God rewards them. He entrusts them with the gifts of the Spirit, He anoints them, and He uses them to do great exploits in His Name.

## Destined for Greatness

"Well, Brother Copeland, you know not everyone is destined for greatness in the kingdom of God. As the Bible says, 'Some vessels are gold and silver, others are soil and earth.' I guess I'm just one of those little mud vessels." If you are, it's your own fault! God isn't the One Who decides if we're to be vessels of honor or not. We make the decision ourselves. As II Timothy 2:19-21 says:

**The Lord knoweth them that are his. And, Let every one that nameth the name of Christ depart from iniquity.**

**But in a great house there are not only vessels of gold and of silver, but also of wood and of earth; and some to honour, and some to dishonour.**

**If a man therefore purge himself from these, he shall be a vessel unto honour, sanctified, and meet for the master's use, and prepared unto every good work.**

Do you want to be a vessel of honor in the house of God? According to that Scripture, you can be if you'll purge yourself from iniquity and dishonor. Notice I said, purge *yourself*. God won't do it for you. He cleansed you from sin the moment you were born again, but it's your responsibility to keep yourself pure. It's up to you to confess your sins and walk in holiness day by day. God will give you the power, certainly, but you're the one who must put that power to work.

Some Christians seem to be sitting around waiting for God to come and jerk the cigarette out of their mouth, stomp on it and say, "That's the last one of those filthy things I'll ever let you smoke." But they are waiting in vain. The Bible doesn't say Jesus will drag you away from iniquity, it says you are to *depart* from it.

According to this verse in II Timothy, if you're a servant, you'll also depart from dishonor. You'll cleanse yourself of the phony faith tactics and other subtly dishonorable practices many believers use.

You won't be like one fellow who went down to the altar at church, knelt down right next to the richest man in the congregation and started praying loudly, in his finest Elizabethan English: "Oh God, Thou knowest how we've suffered in our household because we don't have a washing machine. You know, Lord, how my little babies have to wear dirty diapers because I don't have any way to wash them. Oh God, you know I've given away all I have for you . . ."

When the rich man yielded to the pressure and gave him a washing machine, that fellow said he got it by faith. That wasn't faith! It was a religious con and that's the worst kind of con there is. We must back away from such dishonorable ways. We need to be a people who would rather wash our clothes out by hand than do something like that. We need to be the kind of people who get off in a corner where nobody can hear us and pray to our heavenly Father in secret, believing He will reward us openly!

## Be a Good Soldier

Once you've purged yourself from sin and dishonor, there's something else you must learn to do if you want to qualify as a servant or handmaiden. You can find it in II Timothy 2:3: **"Thou therefore endure hardness, as a good soldier of Jesus Christ."**

Make no mistake about it. There are hardships involved in being a bondservant of God. But there is no hardship, no problem, no suffering, and no onslaught of persecution that can conquer you. Nothing hell can devise is powerful enough to overcome the mighty name of Jesus and the power of the full armor of Almighty God.

You are thoroughly equipped for victory. Yet to win that victory, you will have to go to the battleground. You will have to face the fact that you are a soldier.

Some Christians whine, "I don't feel like fighting the fight of faith today."

That doesn't make any difference. You don't ask a soldier if he'd like to get up and go to combat this morning. You don't say, "Sir, could I bother you for a few moments? I hate to interrupt your checker game, but we're having a war about 10 miles up the road and I just wondered if you'd like to go . . ."

NO! You don't ask a soldier to go to the battlefield, you simply expect him to be there. What's more, a good soldier won't just sit around waiting for the commander to come in with assignments. He'll be there when the plans are being made saying, "Let me be a part of this battle. I want to go."

God is looking for soldiers like that. He is looking for people who are as eager to get in on the action as the boys on my fifth grade football team were. I'll never forget that team. There were about 14 of us and everyone was constantly hanging on the coach's arm begging him to let us in the game. "Put me in there, Coach. I can whip that guy. Just let me have that ball. Nobody can catch me!"

One thing about that bunch of boys, we were eager. We weren't any good but we were ready. If you'll be like that spiritually, God will put you where the action is. He'll give you more excitement than you ever dreamed you'd have. He'll help you turn a shopping center into a revival station if you'll give Him the chance.

> **Nothing hell can devise is powerful enough to overcome the mighty name of Jesus and the power of the full armor of Almighty God.**

## Get Ready!

Finally, as a servant or handmaiden, you need to prepare yourself to bless others instead of always looking to be blessed by someone else. II Timothy 2:6 says, **"The husbandman that laboureth must be first partaker of the fruits."** Eat from your own field of faith. Develop your own prayer life. Quit running around all over the country trying to get somebody else to pray for you all the time.

Don't expect your pastor or any other minister to believe God for you every time you run into trouble. They can't do it. If they try, the great outpouring of the Spirit that's coming will be crippled. You see, God wants to bring millions of people to us to minister to in these last days. They'll be new believers, baby Christians who need help to get healed and delivered.

But if something doesn't change, those new babies will be shoved out of the healing lines by a crowd of overgrown spiritual children who have been running around for 30 years trying to get somebody to counsel them and pray for them. Those of us in the ministry can't let that happen. So you have to grow up and become a bondservant, ready to be used of God—not just using God all the time.

Grow up by putting yourself under the teaching of the Word. Grow up by fellowshiping with people who are students of the Word. Associate with people who have a higher vision than you do and are strong in the Lord.

Then once you've developed your faith, be faithful. Faithfulness is the mark of the handmaidens and servants of God. Revelation 17:14 says,

**The Lamb shall overcome them: for he is Lord of lords, and King of kings: and they that are with him are called, and chosen, and faithful.**

So stay with it. Stay with intercessory prayer. Stay with the Lord. Be faithful to those who need you. Keep the Word of God burning in your heart all the time. Stay ready so that when somebody needs your help, you don't have to go fast and pray. You've already fasted. You've already prayed. You're ready.

This is an hour when we must stay ready 24 hours a day. Like an army, we've been trained over the last few years. We've learned to walk by faith and not by sight, and God has honed us spiritually until we have a keen sword and a keen eye for the battle.

We've fought the battle where our own personal lives are concerned. Now it's time for us to join our forces and fight the battle for this dying, lost, sick world that is going to hell around our feet. It's time for us to lay down our lives and open the way for our God to show wonders in heaven and signs on earth. It's time for us to become the servants and handmaidens of the Lord. ■

**Kenneth Copeland** is President and Founder of *Kenneth Copeland Ministries* in Fort Worth, Texas. For more than 28 years, he has lived committed to teaching believers around the world how to live victorious Christian lives based on the Word of God through the *Believer's Voice of Victory* television broadcasts, books, record albums, Victory campaigns, Believers' Conventions, and the *Believer's Voice of Victory* magazine. The above article was reprinted by permission from Believer's Voice of Victory, Vol. 22, No. 8, August 1994. Copyright ©1994 *Kenneth Copeland Ministries, Inc.* All rights reserved. For a free one-year subscription, write to *Kenneth Copeland Ministries*, Fort Worth, Texas 76192-0001.

# IMPORTANT DISTINCTIONS THAT MAKE A DIFFERENCE

## by Wade E. Taylor

TEACHING

*All Scriptures KJV unless otherwise indicated.*

*Behold, I stand at the door, and knock: IF ANY man [or woman] hear my voice, and open the door, I will come in to him, and will sup with him, and he with me (Revelation 3:20).*

The certainty that all Christians have the "abiding presence" of the Holy Spirit dwelling within them is absolute. There are no conditions to meet, apart from receiving Jesus as Savior. For all who are redeemed, this is a reality that can be depended upon. The Holy Spirit is always faithful in His ministry of maintaining our redemption, and of making Jesus known to us and very real within us.

However, the possibility of having the "manifest presence" of the Lord revealed to us is conditional. For this experience to become a part of our spiritual life, we must be able to recognize His presence, and then be willing to turn aside from all activity in order to wait upon Him.

This ability to recognize His manifest presence, and to be able to rightly respond to it, is dependent upon the development of our spiritual sensitivity and upon our obedience in turning aside in response to His presence whenever He desires to visit us.

We must learn how to open the "door" of our being to Him when He personally comes and seeks to reveal His presence to us. This means that those who desire to have this experience of intimate communion with Him must respond to any indication of His manifest presence, and then promptly turn aside from whatever they are involved in, and acknowledge His presence by inviting Him to come within the room of their spiritual life and activity.

In the Song of Solomon, the Lord purposely made an attempt to visit His bride at a time when it was not convenient for her to respond, and she failed the test. This exposed her spiritual need, and caused her to see what her interests truly were. Through this, He was able to teach her concerning the value and the purpose of His "manifest presence."

When He came and knocked on the door of her heart in order to accomplish all of this, she heard His knock and acknowledged it;

**I sleep, but my heart waketh: it is the voice of my beloved that knocketh, saying, Open to me, my sister, my love, my dove, my undefiled (Song of Solomon 5:2).**

She was comfortably resting in bed and made an excuse as to why she could not respond. **"I have put off my coat; how shall I put it on? I have washed my feet; how shall I defile them?"** (Song of Solomon 5:3). Reluctantly, He departed because of her failure to open the door of her spiritual life to Him, even though her excuse was reasonable.

During the time in which the bride lived, the latch on the door of entrance into a home was located on the inside of the door. It could only be unlatched by reaching through a small hole in the door and unlatching it from within. This provided a limited means of security and protection from wild animals.

The Lord had such a desire to visit with His bride that He reached through this opening in the door toward the latch, but He did not open it, as the door of our heart is always in our control, and can only be opened by us. This action by the Lord deeply stirred the bride toward Him. Later, she testified concerning this: **"My beloved put in His hand by the hole of the door, and my bowels were moved for Him"** (Song of Solomon 5:4).

The Lord will never invade or violate our privacy. We must open the door, He never will. This principle is established in Scripture; **"If any man *hear* my voice, *and open* the door, I will come in to him" (Revelation 3:20).** An action is required on our part before He will manifest, or reveal His presence to us.

When she noticed that His hand was reaching toward the latch as an expression of His desire toward her, she (finally) responded and opened the door to Him.

**I rose up to open to my beloved; and my hands dropped with myrrh, and my fingers with sweetsmelling myrrh, upon the handles of the lock.**

**I opened to my beloved; but my beloved had withdrawn himself, and was gone: my soul failed when he spake: I sought him, but I could not find him; I called him, but he gave me no answer (Song of Solomon 5:5-6).**

Now He will allow her to experience the essential difference between the gifts and the blessings that He is able to leave behind for her to find, and the tremendous value of His "manifest presence." He longs for us to come into the understanding of knowing Him as a person, rather than allowing us to continue knowing Him solely for all of the things that He can provide.

He had reluctantly withdrawn His "manifest presence" from the door of entrance into her spiritual life. However, the anointing, or the result of His presence, had remained upon the lock. When she touched the lock, all of this anointing came onto her hands. She had a handful of the gifts and blessings that He left for her when He departed. Previously, she would have been content to have these apart from Him, but now she panicked and longed for the personal presence of the Bridegroom Himself.

Many are not able to differentiate between these two different aspects of His presence. First, there is the general sense of His divine presence that relates to our salvation and to its outworking within our lives. This speaks of the unconditional "abiding presence" of the Holy Spirit within us.

Second, there is the coming of the Lord to us in order to personally reveal Himself to us, and to share Himself with us in fellowship. This speaks of a conditional visitation from the Lord, and is referred to as His "manifest presence."

The first aspect of His presence is general, and relates to His enabling grace and power. **"Do not I fill heaven and earth? saith the Lord" (Jeremiah 23:24).**

The second aspect of His presence is specific and personal, and relates to His person. **"He standeth behind our wall, he looketh forth at the windows, showing himself through the lattice" (Song of Solomon 2:9).**

Previously, the bride had vividly expressed a characteristic of the Bridegroom; the sensitiveness of His "manifest presence." She had said, **"My beloved is like a roe or a young hart" (Song of Solomon 2:9).** She knew that His manifest presence was delicate, and that it could be easily grieved. Therefore, she should have known that He would leave when she delayed her response to Him.

**I opened to my beloved; but my beloved had withdrawn himself, and was gone: my soul failed when he spake: I sought him, but I could not find him; I called him, but he gave me no answer (Song of Solomon 5:6).**

We should carefully consider these things, and then learn from her mistake. We must be diligent in becoming increasingly more perceptive than we are in discerning His presence. Whenever He comes to reveal Himself to us, we should promptly acknowledge His presence. Then, we should turn aside from whatever we are involved in and, in a spirit of anticipation, invite Him to come within the room of our spiritual being.

After she realized that He was gone, she turned to those who should have been seeking Him with her, and said to them, **"I charge you, O daughters of Jerusalem, if ye find my beloved, that ye tell him, that I am sick of love" (Song of Solomon 5:8).**

There are two different categories of Christians within the church. This is clearly brought out in the Song of Solomon:

**My dove, my undefiled is but one; she is the only one of her mother, she is the choice one of her that bare her. The daughters saw her, and blessed her (Song of Solomon 6:9).**

The first group is the "bride." The bride has captured the singular attention and interest of the Bridegroom. She had said to the Lord,

**Tell me, O thou whom my soul loveth, where thou feedest, where thou makest thy flock to rest at noon: for why should I be as one that turneth aside by the flocks of thy companions? (Song of Solomon 1:7).**

She seeks to go beyond others to the Lord Himself.

The second group are the daughters of Jerusalem. These are saved and have some understanding of the things of God. They regularly attend church and become involved to a certain extent. Their testimony is quite different: **"What is thy beloved more than another beloved, that thou dost so charge us?" (Song of Solomon 5:9).** They are saying, "We have gone far enough, we will stay here. Besides, we do not see why we need to go through all these dealings."

The Lord had withdrawn His "manifest presence" from the bride. However, she was not satisfied with the church program, apart from the presence of the Lord of the program. Therefore, she spoke to the church visible, portrayed here as the daughters of Jerusalem, and said to them, **"I charge you, O daughters of Jerusalem, if ye find my beloved, that ye tell him, that I am sick of love" (Song of Solomon 5:8).**

The daughters of Jerusalem answered her and said,

> **What is thy beloved more than another beloved, O thou fairest among women? What is thy beloved more than another beloved, that thou dost so charge us? (Song of Solomon 5:9).**

They only saw the benefits of being a Christian. To them, going to church represented the doing of their "duty." Also, it provided them with a time for social fellowship and activities. The thought of fellowship and communion with the Lord Himself was far from their minds, or interest.

The daughters of Jerusalem could only say to the bride, "What is He more than a good job, a nice home, or security? What is He more than all of the good things that we have? We are satisfied and content. We ARE the daughters of Jerusalem, and it is enough; do not bother us with your seeking of the Lord. Besides, you are trying to be too spiritual."

But something had happened within the being of the bride. She had experienced the joy and the satisfaction of communion with Him. She had been within the "garden enclosed" with Him. Now, she longed for the continuing experience of His personal presence, and felt incomplete when she was apart from Him.

When the daughters of Jerusalem said to the bride, "What is He more than another," she did not tell them about all of the blessings that she had received from Him. Rather, she began to tell them about the Bridegroom Himself.

> **My beloved is white and ruddy, the chiefest among ten thousand.**
>
> **His head is as the most fine gold, his locks are bushy, and black as a raven.**
>
> **His eyes are as the eyes of doves by the rivers of waters, washed with milk, and fitly set.**
>
> **His cheeks are as a bed of spices, as sweet flowers: his lips like lilies, dropping sweetsmelling myrrh.**
>
> **His hands are as gold rings set with the beryl: his belly is as bright ivory overlaid with sapphires.**
>
> **His legs are as pillars of marble, set upon sockets of fine**

**gold: his countenance is as Lebanon, excellent as the cedars.**

**His mouth is most sweet: yea, he is altogether lovely. This is my beloved, and this is my friend, O daughters of Jerusalem (Song of Solomon 5:10-16).**

She gave an intimate, personal description of her beloved, the Lord Jesus Christ. She was able to clearly describe His Person because she had been spending time alone with Him, and had a single eye toward Him, alone. She knew him, and could give clear expression to His beauty and desirability.

The daughters of Jerusalem had said, **"What is thy beloved more than another beloved, that thou dost so charge us?"** The bride exalted the Lord Jesus and set Him forth as the answer to the inner cry of every heart. This brought a response from the daughters of Jerusalem that is so needed in our day of special gimmicks and programs to build up the church.

**Whither is thy beloved gone, O thou fairest among women? whither is thy beloved turned aside? that we may seek him with thee (Song of Solomon 6:1).**

Their hearts were stirred by the testimony that flowed up out of her being as she expressed her love for Him. The bride set forth the Lord Himself in evident view for the daughters of Jerusalem to behold.

In Acts 1:8 the Lord said, **"But ye shall receive power, after that the Holy Ghost is come upon you: and ye shall be *witnesses unto me . . .*"** As we set our gaze upon Him and "witness unto Him," His beauty is reflected through us for others to behold.

The enemy of our spiritual life will seek to turn us aside from this, and will try to deceive us by telling us, "Do not spend time waiting on the Lord. It is selfish to seek to become personally spiritual. Do not waste your time alone in fellowship with Jesus. Rather, go out and do something for somebody else. Get so busy working for the Lord that you have no time to meet with the Lord in your own devotional life." The enemy knows the power that can flow through the life of one who has been alone with the Lord in His chambers. He knows the heart cry of those who will eagerly respond when they witness the beauty of Jesus being expressed through the life of His bride, who truly knows Him.

We must be willing to set apart time to wait upon Him in His presence, whenever He comes to us for this purpose. As we do this, we will fall so completely in love with Jesus that we will be changed and become like Him. Then, it will be He that is seen rather than us. Then, wherever we go, the result of this "manifest presence," that we have experienced in times of intimate communion with Him, will cut through every bondage and every fear in those who are witnessing the result of our life in His. This will bring others to a knowledge of Jesus Christ.

**Whither is thy beloved gone, O thou fairest among women? whither is thy beloved turned aside? that we may seek him with thee (Song of Solomon 6:1).**

**"For many are called, but few are chosen" (Matthew 22:14).** The "many" refers to the daughters of Jerusalem. The "few" refers to the bride. Another way to say this is: "The daughters of Jerusalem are called, but a bride is being chosen out from among them because she is willing to respond to His presence and to come apart and seek Him."

Here again, two different categories are expressed, the called and the chosen. The "called" includes all Christians. The "chosen" refers to those who are pressing on to know the Lord Himself, and are obediently turning aside to spend time with Him alone, even when it is not convenient for them to do so.

The Lord is calling a bride out from among those who are still saying, "I have gone to bed, how shall I get up?" These "daughters of Jerusalem" know the voice of the Lord to a degree, but they are not committed. They have a limited involvement in the church, but are willing to go only so far and then draw a line and refuse to go further. They say, "I will not become one of those fanatics." The price for going on to truly know His manifest presence is very high, and they are not willing to pay this price.

**"The daughters saw her, and blessed her" (Song of Solomon 6:9).** The daughters of Jerusalem have enough spiritual capacity that they can see the bride, and enough spiritual sense to know that they should bless her. However, they can only know the Lord through the description that the bride gives to them when she, with a glow within her being says to them, **"This is my beloved, and this is my friend, O daughters of Jerusalem" (Song of Solomon 5:16).**

How much better, that we should arise from our bed of indifference and respond to His knocking on the door of our heart and invite Him to come within. Those who do this will never again be content with merely knowing about Him through the knowledge of His omnipresence within the church. These will be progressively drawn upward into the place where they will come to truly and intimately know Him through the ongoing revelation of His manifest presence. ■

**Wade Taylor** is the Founder and Director of *Pinecrest Bible Training Center* in Salisbury Center, New York. Wade is known for his deep and sincere passion for Jesus. This article is an excerpt from his book, **The Secret of the Stairs**, which is an exposition of the Song of Solomon. It can be ordered by sending $7.95 plus $1.75 S/H to Wade Taylor, c/o *Pinecrest BTC*, P. O. Box 320, Salisbury Center, NY 13454-0320.

# TEACHING

# WORDS OF LIFE

by Rick Joyner

*All Scriptures NAS unless otherwise indicated.*

**Death and life are in the power of the tongue, and those who love it will eat its fruit (Proverbs 18:21).**

Words can have a most extraordinary power. In a basic way, the definition of life might be *communication*. To communicate means "to exchange." We determine that something is alive as long as it is able to communicate, or interrelate, with its environment—to breathe the air, partake of food, etc. When this exchange stops, death has come. We refer to creatures according to their ability to communicate; a higher form of life can communicate on a higher level. Jesus said, **"The words that I have spoken to you are *spirit and are life*"** (John 6:63). We have true spiritual life to the degree that our communication with the Lord is developed and maintained. If we have spiritual communication with Jesus, they can kill the body, but they cannot kill us, because our life is on a higher level.

Jesus is the Word of God. He is the Father's communication with the creation. Those who hear His voice are joined to the greatest power in the universe, and it is a power of life. One word from the Lord caused creation to be formed. The Lord did not think and bring forth the creation—He spoke. The Lord did not say, "Think and this mountain will be moved," but, "*Speak* to the mountain" (see Matthew 17:20). Words are the conduit for the greatest power in the universe. The more spiritually mature we become, the more we will understand this.

As we become more closely joined to the Word Himself, the more precious and powerful our words will become. As I heard one preacher say, "It is amazing how few words the Word Himself used." The more valuable a thing is to us, the more careful we will be in handling it. As we comprehend the power and value of words, the more careful we will be with them. The more careful that we are with this great power, the more power the Lord can trust us with.

**Like apples of gold in settings of silver is a word spoken in right circumstances (Proverbs 25:11).**

Words spoken in right circumstances fit perfectly. Words that are spoken out of time can lose their power. *The anointing is connected to timing.* The Lord moves in perfect order and perfect timing, and if we are going to be used to speak His words, we must be sensitive to His timing. His whole life on this earth was a testimony to the grace of timing. He knew exactly when and what to say in every circumstance. He knew that the gentle teaching on living waters would touch the heart of the woman at the well, who was obviously living a life of discontent and unfulfillment. He knew that the teaching on being born again would seize the attention of Nicodemus. Had those teachings been given in the opposite settings they would probably not have had the same impact.

We must recognize that what the Lord is anointing for one person or group may not be what He is anointing for another. When He spoke to the seven churches in Revelation, even though they all existed at the same time and in the same geographic location, they still all needed a different word.

In an exposition of the importance of knowing the language of the Spirit, Paul said:

> **Yet we do speak wisdom among those who are mature; a wisdom, however, not of this age, nor of the rulers of this age, who are passing away;**
>
> **but we speak God's wisdom in a mystery, the hidden wisdom, which God predestined before the ages to our glory;**

> **the wisdom which none of the rulers of this age has understood; for if they had understood it, they would not have crucified the Lord of glory;**
>
> **but just as it is written, "Things which eye has not seen and ear has not heard, and which have not entered the heart of man, all that God has prepared for those who love Him."**
>
> **For to us God revealed them through the Spirit; for the Spirit searches all things, even the depths of God.**
>
> **For who among men knows the thoughts of a man except the spirit of the man, which is in him? Even so the thoughts of God no one knows except the Spirit of God.**
>
> **Now we have received, not the spirit of the world, but the Spirit who is from God, that we might know the things freely given to us by God,**
>
> **which things we also speak, not in words taught by human wisdom, but in those taught by the Spirit, *combining spiritual thoughts with spiritual words*.**
>
> **But a natural man does not accept the things of the Spirit of God; for they are foolishness to him, and he cannot understand them, because they are spiritually appraised.**
>
> **But he who is spiritual appraises all things, yet he himself is appraised by no man.**
>
> **For who has known the mind of the Lord, that he should**

**instruct Him? But we have the mind of Christ (I Corinthians 2:6-16).**

There is a language of the Spirit that transcends human language. It is contrary and offensive to the natural mind of men. This is one reason why the Lord has spoken to men through dreams and visions from the beginning. He is not trying to confuse us by all of the strange symbols and metaphors that are the medium of dreams and visions, but He is trying to teach us the language of the Spirit, which is much greater than human language. It has been said, "A picture is worth a thousand words." In the language of the Spirit this is true. The symbolism of dreams and visions often reveals far more than human language can. This is foolishness to the natural mind, but for those who are spiritual, it is a much higher form of communication.

The primary difference between the languages of men and the language of the Spirit is that the former comes from the mind and the latter comes from the heart. Living waters come from the "innermost being." To share that which will be true life, we must share that which comes from our heart, not just our minds.

The Jewish exorcists in Acts 19:15 knew about Jesus in their minds, but He did not dwell in their hearts. Therefore, when they tried to use His name to drive out darkness, the darkness rose up and drove them out. Demons are spiritual creatures, and they only respond to words that are spirit. For our words to have the power of light to drive out darkness, they must come from our

innermost being. We only have true spiritual authority to the degree that the King dwells within us.

This does not mean that we cannot ever share that which was first given to another—every time we share from the Scriptures we do that—but the words must become "ours." We cannot have a relationship with another person's knowledge of Jesus—He must be our Jesus. True ministry is not just parroting words of knowledge. True ministry is by the Spirit and only the Spirit can beget that which is spiritual.

**And as for you, the anointing which you received from Him abides in you, and you have no need for anyone to teach you; but as His anointing teaches you about all things, and is true and is not a lie, and just as it has taught you, you abide in Him (I John 2:27).**

This does not mean that we do not receive teaching from men, as the Lord gave teachers to His church for that reason, but we must recognize the anointing of the Holy Spirit working through the men. The men on the road to Emmaus were sensitive to the spiritual words spoken to them by Jesus because their hearts burned within them. However, they did not recognize the Lord until they saw Him break the bread. It is when we see Jesus as the one who is breaking our bread, who is teaching us, regardless of whom it comes through, that our eyes, too, will begin to open. It is not by seeing with the eyes of our minds, but with the eyes of our hearts that counts.

## The Power of Truth

The great preacher Charles Spurgeon once lamented that he could find ten men who would die for the Bible for every one who would read it. This ratio is probably still accurate today, and for our other Christian duties as well. We can probably find ten men who will fight for prayer in public schools for every one who actually prays with his own children at home. We may have ten men and women who complain about the sex and violence on television for every one who actually refuses to watch it. This must and will change. Our power to be salt and light in the world does not depend just on what we believe, but on our faithfulness to our beliefs.

**"That which is born of the flesh is flesh, and that which is born of the Spirit is spirit" (John 3:6).** We are utterly dependent on the Holy Spirit for bearing true spiritual fruit. Because the Holy Spirit is "the Spirit of truth," He will only endorse with His presence and power that which is true. The Lord judges our hearts, not our minds. For this reason, "heart religion" is about to take precedence over intellectual religion. However, we must never abandon our commitment to sound biblical truth. The highest levels of power will be given to those who have embraced both the Word and the Spirit.

The great darkness that is now sweeping the world has happened on our watch. The coming great release of power in Christian leadership will be the result of a great repentance and conviction of sin that sweeps over the body of

Christ. Movements that exhort men and women to faithfulness and their spiritual responsibilities will have a profound impact on the whole church. The repentance that resulted from the humiliations of the last decade is also about to bear great fruit.

As the Lord declared, **"Whoever exalts himself shall be humbled; and whoever humbles himself shall be exalted" (Matthew 23:12).** Even though much of the humility has been the result of judgment, the degree to which the church embraced the judgment has prepared her to be lifted up in the esteem of the nations. Even though the attacks and slander will always be with us, the world's esteem for the advancing church is about to rise.

## Only Patience Bears Lasting Fruit

Some consider it a travesty that the New Testament does not take a decisive stand against some of the greatest moral evils of the times in which it was written, such as slavery, abortion and infanticide (the practice of killing babies if they were not the desired sex, or had defects). It is true that the first century leaders of the church did not begin frontal assaults against these great evils. However, it was not because of negligence or irresponsibility—they had a higher strategy with a greater power. They did not just flail at the branches of human depravity—they put the ax to the root of the tree.

With focused, unyielding concentration, the apostles to the early church maintained their frontal assault on sin. They drove back the spirit of death by lifting up the Prince of Life. When the issue of slavery did arise in his letter to Philemon, Paul did not attack the issue of slavery directly, but rose above it by appealing to love and the fact that Onesimus was a brother. This may offend the penchant for militancy that issue-oriented activists usually have, but it is the way of the Spirit. As even the secular historian Will Durant observed, "Caesar tried to change men by changing institutions. Christ changed institutions by changing men."

The way of the Spirit is to penetrate beyond what a frontal assault on issues can usually accomplish. There are times for bold confrontations, but usually the Lord works much slower than we are willing to accept. This is because He is working toward a much deeper, more complete change—working from the inside out, not the outside in.

The divinely powerful weapons are about to be reclaimed and used on an unprecedented scale by the church. As intercessory and spiritual warfare movements continue to mature, the results will become increasingly spectacular. Even so, the most powerful weapon given to the church is *spiritual truth*. Facts can be "truth," but spiritual truth is only found when knowledge is properly combined with life. It is when we live what we believe that we embrace spiritual, eternal truth. As the church begins to live the truth that she knows, her light will increase and shine into the darkness.

Light is more powerful than darkness; love is more powerful than hatred; life is more powerful than death. As we begin to walk in the light, love and life of the Son of God, we will put darkness and death to flight. The power of the church does not lie in her ability to just articulate the truth, but to walk in it. This is the foundation of the great release of power coming to the church.

## The Greater Wisdom

The way of the Spirit is practical. He does want the will of God to be done on earth as it is in heaven. We, too, must be committed to seeing practical fruit. However, our desire not to be so heavenly-minded that we do not do any earthly good has often resulted in our becoming so earthly-minded that we are not doing any spiritual good either. If we impact men spiritually, it will ultimately result in earthly good, but the reverse is not true. If we only impact institutions and outward behavior, we may change the facade of things, but we have not dealt with the roots and they will sprout again.

It is not just bearing fruit that counts, but bearing fruit *that remains*. For us to bear the fruit that is eternal, we must learn patience. We are exhorted to be **"imitators of those who through faith *and* patience inherit the promises" (Hebrews 6:12).** The great wisdom that is about to come upon the church is to see first from the eternal perspective, which will impart the essential ability to plan with strategy and vision for lasting fruit. ∎

TEACHING

# TWO PRINCIPLES OF CONDUCT

by

## Watchman Nee

*All Scriptures KJV unless otherwise indicated.*

God created man, and He Who created man made provision for the sustenance of the man He had created. Man derived his existence from God, and it was God's intention that man should be dependent on Him for his life throughout its entire course. The life He had given was to be nourished by means of suitable food which He Himself supplied.

> **And the LORD God planted a garden eastward in Eden; and there HE put the man whom HE had formed.**
>
> **And out of the ground made the LORD God to grow every tree that is pleasant to the sight, and good for food; the tree of life also in the midst of the garden, and the tree of knowledge of good and evil (Genesis 2:8-9).**

Through these two trees God has shown us in figure two different ways in which people may spend their days on earth; the principle that governs the conduct of some is the knowledge of good and evil, while others are governed by the principle of life.

Let us spend a little time considering these two different principles as they affect the lives of God's children: and let us note at the outset that while Christians may be governed mainly by the one principle or the other, not all the actions of the same Christian are invariably regulated by the same principle.

## What Is the Principle of Good and Evil?

If our conduct is controlled by the principle of good and evil, then whenever we have to make a decision we first enquire: Is this right, or is it wrong? Would it be good to do this, or would it be evil? Many Christians hesitate before doing anything and turn such questions round and round in their minds. They are bent on doing the right thing: they wish to avoid all evil: they want to live a life in keeping with what they consider to be Christianity: so they scrupulously weigh all their actions. They carefully examine each situation they meet, and not until they are persuaded that a certain course of action is good will they go ahead.

They seek to act in a way that befits a Christian, so they are always on the alert to select the right from the wrong and to do only what they consider to be right.

But God's Word says:

**The tree of the knowledge of good and evil, thou shalt not eat of it: for in the day that thou eatest thereof thou shalt surely die (Genesis 2:17).**

To act according to the seemingly lofty standard of rejecting all that is bad and choosing only the good is not Christianity. That is living under the law: it is acting according to the Old Covenant, not the New. To act in this way is to conform to religious or ethical standards: it falls altogether short of the Christian standard.

## Christianity Is Based on Life

What is Christianity? Christianity is a matter of life. If you are a Christian, then you possess *a new life*; and when you have to decide on a course of action, you do not ask, Would it be right to do this? You ask, *If I do this, how will it affect my inner life*? How will that new life within me react to this? It is a most amazing thing that the objective of so many Christians is only conformity to an *external standard*, though what God has given us by new birth is not a lot of new rules and regulations to which we are required to conform. He has not brought us to a new Sinai and given us a new set of commandments with their "Thou shalt" and "Thou shalt not." Christianity does not require that we investigate the rights and wrongs of alternative courses of action, but *that we test the reaction of the divine life to any proposed course.* As a Christian you now possess the life of Christ,

and it is the reactions of His life that you have to consider. If, when you contemplate any move, there is a *rise of life within you* to make that move; if there is a *positive response* from the inner life; if there is *"the anointing"* within (see I John 2:20, 27); then you can confidently pursue the proposed course. The inner life has indicated that. But if, when you contemplate a certain move, the inner life begins *to languish*, then you may know that the move you contemplated *should be avoided*, however commendable it may seem to be.

Do realize that the conduct of many a non-Christian is governed by the principle of right and wrong. Wherein does the Christian differ from the non-Christian if the same principle governs both? God's Word shows us plainly that the Christian is controlled by *the life of Christ*, not by any *external code* of ethics. There is something vital within the Christian that responds to what is of God and reacts against what is not of Him; so we must take heed to our inner reactions. When the living spring within us wells up in response to any suggestion, we should follow that; but when it declines, we should repudiate the idea. We dare not be governed by externalities, nor by reasonings, our own or other peoples'. Others may approve a certain thing, and when we weigh up the pros and cons we too may think it right; but what is the inner life saying about it?

Once you realize that the determining factor in all Christian conduct is life, then you know that you must not only avoid all that is evil, but also all that is just *externally good*. Only what issues from the Christian life is Christian conduct;

therefore we cannot consent to any action that does not spring from life. Let us remember God's Word: **"Of the tree of the knowledge of good and evil, thou shalt not eat of it: for in the day that thou eatest thereof thou shalt surely die."** Note that **"good and evil"** are set together here, and over against **"good and evil"** is set **"life."** The standard of life is a transcendent standard.

In my early Christian days I sedulously sought to avoid all that was evil and deliberately set myself to do what was good. And I seemed to be making splendid progress. At that time I had a fellow-worker who was two years older than I, and we two were always disagreeing. The differences that arose between us were not concerning our own personal affairs; our disagreements were about public matters and our disputes were public, too. I used to say to myself: If he wants to do that bit of work in such-and-such a way I shall protest, for it is not right. But no matter how I protested, he always refused to give way. I had one line of argument—right and wrong: he also had one line of argument —his seniority. No matter how I might reason in support of my views, he invariably reasoned that he was two years older than I. However many irrefutable evidences I might produce to prove that he was wrong and I was right, he produced his one unvarying evidence to justify every course of action he adopted—he was two years older than I. How could I refute that fact? So he always won the day. He gained his point outwardly, but inwardly I never gave way. I resented his unreasonableness and still clung firmly to my contention that he was wrong and I was right. One day I brought my grievance to an elderly sister in the Lord who had a wealth of spiritual experience. I explained the case, brought forth my arguments, then appealed to her to arbitrate. Was he right or was I?—That was what I wanted know. She seemed to ignore all the rights and wrongs of the situation, and looking me straight in the face, just answered quietly, "You'd better do as he says." I was thoroughly dissatisfied with her answer and thought to myself: If I'm right, why not acknowledge that I'm right? If I'm wrong, why not tell me I'm wrong? Why tell me to do what he says? So I asked, "Why?" "Because," she said, "in the Lord the younger should submit to the older." "But," I retorted, "in the Lord, if the younger is right and the older wrong, must the younger still submit?" At that time I was a high school student and had learned nothing of discipline, so I gave free vent to my annoyance. She simply smiled and said once more: "You'd better do as he says."

At a later date there was to be a baptismal service and three of us were to bear responsibility together—the brother who was two years older than I, a brother who was seven years older than he, and myself. Now let's see what will happen, I thought. I always have to do what you, who are my senior by two years, tell me:

> *To act according to the seemingly lofty standard of rejecting all that is bad and choosing only the good is not Christianity.*

will you always do what this brother, who is your senior by seven years, tells you? Together we three discussed the work, but he refused to accept any suggestion put forward by his senior: at every point he insisted on having his own way. Finally he dismissed us both with the remark: "You two just leave things to me; I can manage quite well alone." I thought, What kind of logic is this? You insist that I always obey you because you are my senior, but you need never obey your senior. Forthwith I sought out the elderly sister, spread the matter before her, and asked for her verdict on the case. "The thing that annoys me," I said, "is that that brother has no place for right and wrong." She rose to her feet and asked: "Have you, right up to this present day, *never seen what the life of Christ is*? These past few months you keep asserting that you are right and your brother is wrong. Do you not know the meaning of the Cross?" Since the one issue I raised was the issue of right or wrong, she met me on my own ground and asked: "Do you think it right for you to behave as you have been doing? Do you think it right for you to talk as you have been talking? Do you think it right for you to come and report these matters to me? You may be acting reasonably and rightly; but even if you are, *what about your inner registrations? Does the life within you not protest against your own behavior?"* I had to admit that even when I was right by human standards, *the inner life* pronounced me wrong.

The Christian standard not only passes its verdict on what is not good, but also on that which is mere external goodness. Many things are right according to human standards, but the divine standard pronounces them wrong because they lack the divine life. On the day to which I have just referred I saw for the first time that if I was to live *in the presence of God*, then all my conduct must be governed by the *principle of life*, not by the principle of right and wrong. From that day I began to see more and more clearly that in relation to any course of action, even if others pronounced it right, and I myself considered it right, and every aspect of the case indicated that it was right, I must still be very sensitive to the reactions of the life of Christ within me. As we advance in the approved course, does the inner life grow stronger or weaker? Does the inner "anointing" confirm the rightness of the course, or does an absence of the "anointing" indicate that the divine approval is withheld? God's way for us is not known by *external indications* but by *internal*

---

**✸ Mustard Seeds of Wisdom**

Our whole peace in this life consists rather in humble sufferance than in not feeling adversities. Whosoever knows best how to suffer will keep the greatest peace. That man is conqueror of himself, and lord of the world, the friend of Christ, and heir of Heaven.

*– Thomas A' Kempis*

*registrations*. It is peace and joy in the spirit that indicate the Christian's path.

When I was visiting a certain place, a brother who was exceedingly critical of the place was a guest there, too. He knew the place had much to offer spiritually, but he disapproved of very much that was done there and was constantly making adverse comparisons with the place from which he came. During the two or three months we were there together his criticisms exceeded those of everyone else. One day he went altogether too far, so I said to him: "Why ever do you remain here? Why not pack up and leave?" "The reason lies here," he answered, pointing to his heart. "Every time I prepare to go, my peace of heart goes. Once I actually departed, and I stayed away for a fortnight, but I had to ask to be allowed to return." "Brother," I said, "can't you see these two different lines of conduct—that which is determined by life and that which is determined by right and wrong?" "Oh!" he said, "not once or twice merely, but a number of times I have sought to leave here, and every time my experience has been the same; as soon as I prepare to go there is an inner forbidding. Even if much that is done here is wrong, for me to leave is also wrong." This brother saw that if there was much spiritual help to be gained in that place, then his only way was to remain there and meet God.

## *Divine Life*

One of the most serious misconceptions among the children of God is that actions are determined by right and wrong. They do what their eyes tell them is right: they do what their background tells them is right: they do what their *years of experience* tell them is right. For a Christian, every decision should be based on the inner life, and that is something totally different from all else. I yearn that you should come to see that a Christian should arrive at no decision other than that which is dictated by life. If the life within you rises to do a thing, then it is right for you to do it: if the life within shrinks back when you advance, then you should immediately call a halt.

I can recall going to a certain place where the brothers were working to real effect. God was truly using them. If you were to ask: Was their work perfect? I should have to answer, No, there was lots of room for improvement. In great humility they asked me to point out anything I saw that was not correct, so I pointed out this and that. But no change took place. Was I annoyed? Not at all. I could only indicate external matters that called for adjustment: I could not see what God was doing inwardly, and it would have been folly on my part to touch that. I dared not advise God what to do in their lives.

In another place I visited, the brothers were not preaching the gospel. They discussed the matter with me and asked if I did not think they ought to be doing so. "Doctrinally you certainly ought," I answered. They admitted that they felt the same, but the surprising thing was that God did not give them the life to do so. Under such circumstances, if we know God, we can only stand aside in silence, for our pathway is governed by His life alone, not by right and wrong. Brothers and Sisters, the contrast between these two principles of life is immense. So many people are still questioning: "Is it right for me to do this? Would it be wrong for me to do that?" The one question for the Christian to ask is, Does the divine life within me rise or fall when I contemplate this thing? The reaction of the divine life within me must determine the course I follow at every point. This is a heart matter.

## "Hear Him"

On the Mount of Transfiguration Moses was present, representing the law; and Elijah was present, representing the prophets. The legal standard was there; and the prophetic standard was there too: but the two who throughout the Old Testament dispensation were qualified to speak were put to silence by God—"This is my beloved Son"; He said, "hear ye Him." Today the standard for the Christian is neither the law nor the prophets; it is Christ, the Christ Who dwells within us: therefore the question is not, Am I right or am I wrong? but, Does the divine life in me acquiesce to this? We shall often find that what we ourselves approve, the life within us disapproves. When that is so, we cannot do what we thought right.

## The Divine Life Must Be Satisfied

I recall a story of two brothers who both cultivated paddy-fields. Their fields were half way up the hill: others were lower down. In the great heat they drew water by day and went to sleep at night. One night, while they were sleeping, the farmers lower down the hill dug a hole in the irrigation channel surrounding the brothers' fields and let all the water flow down on their own fields. Next morning the brothers saw what had happened, but said nothing. Again they filled the troughs with water, and again all the water was drawn off the following night. Still no word of protest was uttered when the next day dawned and they discovered what a mean trick the same farmers had played on them. Were they not Christians? Ought not Christians to be patient? This game was repeated seven nights in succession, and for seven days in succession these two brothers silently suffered the wrong. One would have thought that Christians who could allow themselves to be treated like that day after day, and never utter a word of reproach, would surely be overflowing with joy. Strange to say, they were not happy at all, and their unhappiness distressed them to such an extent that they brought the matter to a brother who was in the Lord's service. Having stated their case, they asked him: "How does it come about that, having suffered all this wrong for a full week, we are still unhappy?" This brother had some experience and he replied: "You're unhappy because you've not gone the full length. You should first irrigate those farmers' fields and then irrigate your own. You go back and test it out, and see whether or not your hearts find rest." They agreed to try, and off they went. Next morning they were afoot earlier than ever, and their first business was to irrigate the fields of those farmers who had so persistently robbed their fields of water. And this amazing thing happened—the more they labored on their persecutors' land, the happier they became. By the time they had finished watering their own land their hearts were at perfect rest. When the brothers had repeated this for two or three days, the farmers called to apologize and added: "If this is Christianity, then we want to hear more about it."

Here we see the difference between the principle of right and wrong and the principle of life. Those two brothers had been most patient: was that not right? They had labored in the intense heat to irrigate their paddy-fields and without a word of complaint had suffered others to steal their water: was that not very good? What then was lacking that they had no peace of heart? They had done what was right: they had done what was good: they had done all that man could require of them: but God was not satisfied. They had no peace of heart because they had not met the demands of His life. When they conformed to His standard, joy and peace welled up in their hearts. The demands of the divine life must be met, so we dare not stop short of God's satisfaction.

What is the Sermon on the Mount? What is taught us in Matthew chapters 5-7? Is it not this, that we dare not be satisfied with anything less than that which meets the demands of the life that God has put within us? The Sermon on the Mount does not teach that, provided we do what is right, then all is well. Man would say: If anyone smites you on the one cheek, why present the other? Surely you have attained the utmost degree of forbearance if you take such an offense

*The demands of the divine life must be met, so we dare not stop short of God's satisfaction.*

without retort. But God says otherwise. If, when you are smitten on the one cheek, you do no more than bow your head and depart, you will find that the inner life will not be satisfied. There will be no inner satisfaction till you turn the other cheek to the smiter for the same treatment. To do so will prove that there is no resentment within. That is the way of life.

Many people say that Matthew 5-7 is too difficult; it is beyond us. I admit it is. It is a sheer impossibility. But here is the point—you have an inner life, and that life tells you that unless you do as the Sermon on the Mount requires, you will find no rest. The whole question lies here, are you walking in the way of life or in the way of good and evil?

Sometimes a brother acts very foolishly. You feel his actions call for strong exhortation or even serious reproof, so one day you set out for his home. Yes, you must give him a good talking-to: that is only right: he has been very wrong. You reach the door: you raise your hand to the doorbell: just as you are about to ring, your hand falls limp by your side. But, you ask, isn't it right to talk to him? The question is not whether it's right to talk to him, but whether the divine life within you allows you to do so. You may exhort that brother, and he may receive your exhortation with courtesy and promise to do what God says, but the more you preach to him the more the life within you wilts. When you return home you will have to admit, I have done wrong.

One day I met a needy brother. He was extremely poor and there was no prospect of help coming to him from any direction, so I thought I certainly must do something for him. Just at that point I myself had no superabundance, so it was at great sacrifice that I came to his aid. I should have been full of joy when I parted with my much-needed money, but the reverse was the case. I felt lifeless, and a voice within said: You were not acting in life; you were just acting on the ground of natural kindness and responding to human need. God did not ask that of you. When I reached home I had to confess my sin and ask His forgiveness.

## Our Actions Must Be Controlled By Life

Brothers and Sisters, let me repeat that all our conduct must be determined, not by good and evil, but by the life within. If you act apart from the requirement of that life, even if what you do is good, you will meet with the divine reproof. We need to discern between life and death. If what I have done has sapped my inner life,

however good the deed may be, I shall have to acknowledge my sin before God and seek His pardon. In I Corinthians 4:4 Paul said: **"I know nothing by myself; yet am I not hereby justified: but he that judgeth me is the Lord."** It is easy to distinguish between good and evil, but Paul was not governed by good and evil: even when he was unaware of having done anything wrong, he still did not dare affirm that all was right with him: he acknowledged that the Lord was his judge. At the judgment seat it is the Lord Who will judge us, but His life is in us now and is directing our way. For that reason Paul said in II Corinthians 5:7, *"We walk by faith, not by sight."* We do not come to decisions on the basis of an outward, legal standard, but on the basis of an inner life. It is a fact that the Lord Jesus Christ dwells within the believer, and He is constantly expressing Himself in us, so we must become sensitive to His life and learn to discern what that life is saying. A great change will take place in us when our conduct is no longer governed by the principle of good and evil but only by the *principle of life*. ■

**Watchman Nee** has long been recognized as one of the most influential writers of our time. His classics that have been translated from Chinese into English include *The Normal Christian Life*, *The Spiritual Man* and *The Release of the Spirit*. His writings cover such diverse topics as distinguishing between spirit, soul and body, intercession, spiritual life and spiritual warfare. *Release of the Spirit* is available through *MorningStar* or your local bookstore.

**PROPHECY**

# THE EYES MUST BE SINGLE

by

## Rick Joyner

*All Scriptures NAS unless otherwise indicated.*

In Isaiah 29:10 the prophets are called the "eyes." That is the function of the prophet, to be the eyes of the body. They are given for vision so that the church may go forward without stumbling, and keep upon the path to which she has been called. It is not impossible for one to stay on the path when blind, but the journey will at best be much more difficult and dangerous, not to mention slow.

Many blind people have done a remarkable job at adjusting to their blindness. They learn to trust their other senses more, and often live very productive lives. However, you will probably not find one blind person anywhere in the world who would not rather have their sight. Likewise, many churches have adjusted to not having the prophetic ministry operating, and are still quite productive. Even so, how much more productive would they be with a mature prophetic ministry operating? How much less would they trip over unforeseen obstacles? How much less would they get blind-sided by the enemy? With how much more resolve and speed could they move along their appointed course? Without question, being sighted does make almost everything we do much easier.

Until the prophets have taken their rightful place in the ministry, the church will continue to grope, stumble, and be subject to difficulties and dangers that are not necessary. As the Lord said in Luke 11:34: **"The light of the body is the eye: therefore when thine eye is *single*, thy whole body is also full of light"** (KJV). We should not settle for anything less than having the whole body full of light, but we must also understand that this requires that the **"eye is single,"** or in unity. Isaiah 52:8 foretells the coming prophetic unity:

> **Your watchmen shall lift up their voices, with their voices they shall sing together; for they**

shall see eye to eye [together] when the Lord brings back Zion (NKJV).

It would be hard to walk if one of your eyes focused on one thing and the other on something else. Presently, the many prophetic voices are often in conflict with each other; but we can trust Isaiah's word that it will not always be that way. The emerging prophetic ministry is maturing fast, and it does seem to be coming into unity even much faster than the church at large. Many prophets are gathering in various places and learning to walk together. This is very encouraging, but the groundwork for single vision must be addressed on an individual basis. We must each address the things that can blur or obscure our vision.

First, if we are going to function as the eye of the body, we must be careful how we use our own eyes. In this Job showed great wisdom: **"I have made a covenant with my eyes; how then could I gaze at a virgin?" (Job 31:1).** Job made a covenant with his eyes not to look upon something that would

cause him to stumble. If our eye is single, upon the Lord, our whole body will be full of light. We can let light and darkness into our soul through our eyes. If we are going to function as eyes for the Lord's body, we must give our eyes to Him, being careful not to look upon those things which would let darkness into our soul. Lust is one of the primary destroyers of prophetic vision. Lust is ultimate, basic selfishness, the exact opposite of the nature of the Lord and the nature of the true prophetic ministry.

In Ephesians 1:18-19 Paul said,

**I pray that the eyes of your heart may be enlightened, so that you may know what is the hope of His calling, what are the riches of the glory of His inheritance in the saints,**

**and what is the surpassing greatness of His power toward us who believe. These are in accordance with the working of the strength of His might.**

To be prophetic, we must have the eyes of our hearts opened, not the eyes

---

**✸ Mustard Seeds of Wisdom**

Satan will not continue to assault you if the circumstances he designed to destroy you are now working to perfect you!

— *Francis Frangipane*

Definition of an old-timer: One who remembers when charity was a virtue and not an organization.

— *Anonymous*

---

of our minds. The primary way that this happens is when we focus upon the Lord—*His calling*, not just our own; the glory of *His inheritance*, not just our own; and the surpassing greatness of *His power*. We will only have true prophetic vision to the degree that we are looking through His eyes.

We must also see more clearly with the eyes of our heart than we do with our physical eyes. What we see in the spirit realm must be more real to us than what we see in the natural realm. Abraham was a prophet and a great example of one whose vision in his heart was more powerful than what he could see with his natural eyes. He left the greatest culture on earth because he was looking for the city that God was building. He saw into the future and lived by that vision just as if it were the present. As the Lord Jesus Himself confirmed, **"Your father Abraham rejoiced to see My day, and he saw it and was glad" (John 8:56).**

It was because Abraham had seen the day of the Lord and the resurrection that he could so easily sacrifice his son Isaac. He knew that his son would be raised from the dead and live forever. Abraham was not living for the temporary realm, but for eternity. This is the

✴ ✴ ✴

*Until the prophets have taken their rightful place in the ministry, the church will continue to grope, stumble and be subject to difficulties and dangers that are not necessary.*

calling for all believers, but it is an especially essential foundation for all who would be prophetic, who are called to help raise the church up to what she is called.

To be prophetic we must live in a different realm. We cannot just see people as they are, but as they are called to be. We cannot just see the church in her present state, but as she is called to become. We must often see the things that are not as though they were, and prophesy the reality of God's future plan and destiny. Every true prophet must pass the test of Ezekiel 37. What do we see in the present valley of dry bones? Those without prophetic vision will only see death. The true prophet can see in even the driest bones an exceedingly great army, and will prophesy life to those bones.

Coming into true unity will not happen just by our getting together, but we must all be beholding the One in Whom all things hold together by the word of *His power*. Anyone can see Babylon, but who can see the city that God is building? That takes prophetic vision to see beyond the way things are, to the One in Whom everything in heaven and earth will be summed up. ∎

PROPHECY

# THE HORDES OF HELL ARE MARCHING
## PART II

### by

### Rick Joyner

*This is Part II of a panoramic dream and vision I received in early 1995. This is obviously allegorical, as are most dreams and visions. I have tried to be faithful to what I actually saw and experienced. It is highly recommended that you read Part I before reading this section. Without reading the first part (included in the previous edition of the Journal), a number of the most important elements in this one may be hard to understand.*

We stood in the Garden of God under the Tree of Life. It seemed that the entire army was there, kneeling before the Lord Jesus. He had just given us the charge to return to the battle for the sake of our brothers who were still bound, and for the world that He still loved. It was both a wonderful and a terrible command. It was wonderful just because it came from Him. It was terrible because it implied that we would have to leave His manifest presence, and the Garden that was more beautiful than anything I had ever seen before. To leave all of this to go into battle seemed incomprehensible.

The Lord continued His exhortation: "I have given you spiritual gifts and power, and an increasing understanding of My word and My kingdom, but the greatest weapon that you have been given is the Father's love. As long as you walk in My Father's love you will never fail. The fruit of this tree is the Father's love which is manifested in Me. This love which is in Me must be your daily bread."

The Lord was not what we might consider to be of a strikingly handsome appearance, but was rather ordinary. Even so, the grace with which He moved and spoke made Him the most attractive person I had ever seen. He was beyond human definition in dignity and nobility. No painting that has sought to capture what He looked like could ever do it, but somehow most of them do resemble Him. I began to think of how He was everything that the Father loves and esteems. He truly is full of grace and truth, to the point that it seemed that nothing but grace and truth should ever matter.

When I ate the fruit from the Tree of Life, the thought of every good thing I had ever known seemed to fill my soul. When Jesus spoke it was the same, only magnified. I never wanted to leave this place. I remembered how I had once thought it must have been boring for those angels who did nothing but worship Him before the throne. Now I knew that there was nothing more wonderful or exhilarating than simply worshiping Him. That would surely be the best part of heaven. It was hard to believe that I had struggled so much with boredom during worship services. I knew that it was only because I had been almost completely out of touch with reality during those times.

## Worship in Spirit and Truth

I was almost overwhelmed with the desire to go back and make up those times during worship when I had allowed my mind to wander, or had occupied myself with other things. The desire to express my adoration for Him became almost uncontrollable. I had to praise Him! As I opened my mouth I was shocked by the spontaneous worship that erupted from the entire army at the same time. I had almost forgotten that anyone else was there, but we were all in perfect unity. The glorious worship could not be expressed in human language.

As we worshiped, a golden glow began to emanate from the Lord. Then there was silver around the gold. Then colors, the richness of which I have never seen with my natural eyes, enveloped us all. With this glory I entered a realm of emotion that I had never experienced before. Somehow I understood that this glory had been there all along, but when we focused on Him the way that we did in worship, we simply began to see more of His glory. The more intensely we worshiped, the more glory we beheld. If this was heaven, it was much, much better than I had ever dreamed.

## Finding His Dwelling Place

I have no idea how long this worship lasted. It could have been minutes or it could have been months. There was simply no way to measure time in that kind of glory. For a time I closed my eyes because the glory I was seeing with my heart was as great as what I was seeing with my physical eyes. When I opened my eyes I was surprised to see that the Lord was not there any longer, but a troop of angels was standing where He had been. One of them stepped up to me and said, "Close your eyes again." When I did, I beheld the glory of the Lord again and was greatly relieved.

Then the angel explained, "What you see with the eyes of your heart is more real than what you see with your physical eyes." I had myself made this statement many times, but how little I had truly walked in it! The angel continued, "It was for this reason that the Lord told His first disciples that it was better for Him to go away so that the Holy Spirit could come. The Lord dwells within you. You have taught this many times, but now you must live it, for you have eaten of the Tree of Life."

The angel then began to lead me back to the gate. I protested that I did not want to leave. Looking surprised, the angel took me by the shoulders and looked me in the eyes. That is when I recognized him as the angel, Wisdom. "You never have to leave this garden. This garden is in your heart because the Creator Himself is within you. You have desired the best part, to worship and sit in His presence forever, and it will never be taken from you."

I acknowledged what Wisdom had said, and then looked past him at the fruit on the Tree of Life. I had a compulsion to grab all that I could before leaving. Knowing my thoughts, Wisdom gently shook me. "No. Even this fruit, gathered in fear, would rot. This fruit and this tree are within you because He is in you. You must believe."

I closed my eyes and tried to see the Lord again but couldn't. When I opened my eyes Wisdom was still staring at me. With great patience he continued, "You have tasted of the heavenly realm, and no one ever wants to go back to the battle once they do. No one ever wants to leave the manifest presence of the Lord. When the apostle Paul came here he struggled for the rest of his life as to whether he should stay and labor for the Lord, or return here to enter into his inheritance; but his inheritance was magnified the longer he stayed. Now that you have the heart of a true worshiper you will always want to be here, and you can when you enter into true worship. The more focused you are on Him, the more glory you will see, regardless of where you are."

Wisdom's words had finally calmed me. Again I closed my eyes just to thank the Lord for this wonderful experience, and the life He had given to me. As I did, I started to see His glory again, and all of the emotion of the previous worship experience flooded my soul. The Lord's words to me were so loud and clear that I was sure they were audible; "I will never leave or forsake you."

"Lord, forgive my unbelief," I responded. "Please help me to never leave or forsake you."

## Walking With Wisdom

As I opened my eyes, Wisdom was still gripping my shoulders. "I am the primary gift that has been given to you for your work," he said. "I will show you the way, and I will keep you on it, but only love will keep you faithful. The highest wisdom is to love the Lord."

Then Wisdom released me and started to walk toward the gate. I followed with ambivalence. I remembered the exhilaration of the battle and the climb up the mountain, and it was compelling, but there was no comparison to the presence of the Lord and the worship I had just experienced. Leaving this would be the greatest sacrifice I had ever made. Then I remembered how it was all inside of me, amazed that I could even forget that so quickly. I began to think about the great battle that was raging within me, between what I saw with my physical eyes and what I saw with my heart.

I moved forward so that I was walking beside Wisdom, and asked, "I have prayed for 25 years to be caught up into the third heaven as Paul had. Is this the third heaven?"

"This is part of it," he replied, "but there is much more."

"Will I be allowed to see more?" I asked.

"You will see much more. I am taking you to see more now," he replied.

I started thinking of the Book of Revelation. "Was John's revelation part of the third heaven?" I asked.

"Part of John's revelation was from the third heaven, but most of it was from the second heaven. The first heaven was before the fall of man. The second heaven is the spiritual realm during the reign of evil upon the earth. The third heaven is when the love and domain of the Father will again prevail over the earth through your King."

"What was the first heaven like?" I inquired, strangely feeling a cold chill as I asked.

"It is wisdom not to be concerned about that now," my companion responded with increased seriousness as my question seemed to jolt him. "Wisdom is to seek to know the third heaven just as you have. There is much more to know about the third heaven than you can know in this life, and it is the third heaven, the kingdom, that you must preach in this life. In the ages to come you will be told about the first heaven, but it is not profitable for you to know at this time."

I resolved to remember the cold chill I had just felt, and Wisdom nodded, which I knew to be an affirmation to that thought. "What a great companion you are," I had to say as I was just flooded with appreciation for this angel. "You really will keep me on the right path."

"I will indeed," he replied.

I was sure I felt love coming from this angel, which was unique, since I had never felt this from other angels, which showed more of a concern out of duty than love. Wisdom responded to my thoughts as if I had spoken them out loud.

"It is wisdom to love and I could not be Wisdom if I did not love you. It is also wisdom to behold the kindness *and* the severity of God. It is wisdom to love Him and fear Him. You are in deception to do otherwise. This is the next lesson that you must learn," he said with unmistakable earnest.

"I do know that, and have taught it many times," I responded, feeling for the first time that maybe Wisdom did not fully know me.

"I have been your companion for a very long time, and I know your teachings," Wisdom replied. "Now you are about to learn what some of your own teachings mean. As you have said many times, 'It is not by believing in your mind, but in your heart that results in righteousness.' "

I apologized, feeling a bit ashamed at having even questioned Wisdom. He graciously accepted my apology. It was then that I realized I had been questioning and challenging him most of my life, often to my injury.

## The Other Half of Love

"There are times to adore the Lord," Wisdom continued, "and there are times to honor Him with the greatest fear and respect. Just as there is a time to plant, and a time to reap, and it is wisdom to know the time for each. True wisdom knows the times and seasons of God. I brought you here because it was time to worship the Lord in the glory of His love. I am now taking you to another place because it is time for you to worship Him in the fear of His judgment. Until you know both we can be separated from each other."

"Do you mean that if I had stayed back there in that glorious worship I would have lost you?" I asked in disbelief.

"Yes. I would have always visited with you when I could, but we would have rarely crossed paths. It is hard to leave such glory and peace, but that is not the whole revelation of the King. He is both the Lion of Judah and the Lamb. To the spiritual children He is the Lamb. To the maturing He is the Lion. To the fully mature He is both the Lion and the Lamb. You have known this in your mind, and I have heard you teach it, but now you will know it in your heart, for you are about to experience the judgment seat of Christ."

## The Return to the Battle

Before leaving the gates to the Garden I asked Wisdom if I could just sit for a while to ponder all that I had just experienced. "Yes, you should do this," he replied, "but I have a better place for you to do it."

I followed Wisdom out of the gates and we began to descend down the mountain. To my surprise the battle was still going on, but not nearly as intensely as it was when we ascended. There were still arrows of accusation and slander flying about on the lower levels, but most of the enemy horde that was left was furiously attacking the great white eagles. The eagles were easily prevailing.

We kept descending until we were almost at the bottom. Just above the levels of "Salvation" and "Sanctification" was the level "Thanksgiving and Praise." I remembered this level very well because one of the greatest attacks of the enemy came as I first tried to reach it. Once we got here the rest of the climb was much easier, and if an arrow got through your armor it healed much faster.

As soon as the enemy spotted me on this level (the enemy could not see Wisdom), a shower of arrows began to rain down on me. I so easily knocked them down with my shield that the enemy quit shooting. Their arrows were now almost gone and they could not afford to waste any more.

The soldiers who were still fighting from this level looked at me in astonishment with a deference that made me very uncomfortable. It was then that I first noticed that the glory of the Lord was emanating from my armor and shield. I told them to climb to the top of the mountain without stopping and they, too, would see the Lord. As soon as they agreed to go they saw Wisdom. They started to fall down to worship him, but he restrained them, and sent them on their way.

## The Faithful

I was filled with love for these soldiers, many of whom were women and children. Their armor was a mess, and they were covered in blood, but they had not quit. In fact, they were still cheerful and encouraged. I told them that they were deserving of more honor than I was, because they had borne the greatest burden of the battle, and had held their ground. They seemed not to believe me, but appreciated that I would say it. However, I really felt that it was true.

Every level on the mountain had to be occupied or the vultures that were left would come and foul it with vomit and excrement until it was difficult to stand on. Most of the ledges were occupied by soldiers which I recognized to be from different denominations or movements which emphasized the truth of the level they were defending. I was embarrassed by the attitude I had maintained toward some of these groups. I had considered some of them out of touch and backslidden at best, but here they were fighting faithfully against a terrible onslaught of the enemy. Their defense of these positions had probably enabled me to keep climbing as I had.

Some of these levels were situated so that there was a view of a good part of the mountain or battlefield, but some were so isolated that the soldiers on them could only see their own position, and seemed not to even know about the rest of the battle raging. They were often so wounded from the slander and accusations that they would be resistant when someone came down to them from a higher level and encouraged them to climb higher. However, when some began to come down from the top reflecting the glory of the Lord, they listened with great joy, and soon began to climb themselves with courage and resolve. As I beheld all of this, Wisdom did not say much, but he seemed very interested in my reactions.

## Reality Discovered

I watched as many soldiers who had been to the top began descending to all of the levels to relieve those who had been taking their stand on those truths. As they did, each level began to shine with the glory they carried. Soon the whole mountain was beginning to shine with a glory that was blinding to the vultures and demons that were left. Soon there was so much glory that the mountain began to have the same feel as the Garden.

I started thanking and praising the Lord and immediately I was in His presence again. It was hard to contain the emotions and glory that was flooding my innermost being. The experience became so intense that I stopped. Wisdom was standing beside me. Putting his hand on my shoulder he said, "You enter His gates with thanksgiving, His courts with praise."

"But that was so real! I felt like I was there again," I exclaimed.

"You were there," replied Wisdom. "It has not gotten more real, but you have. Just as the Lord told the thief on the cross, *'Today' you will be with Me in Paradise,* you can enter Paradise at anytime. The Lord, His Paradise, and this mountain, are all abiding in you, because He is in you. What were but foretastes before are now a reality to you because you have climbed the mountain. The reason that you can see me and others cannot is not because I have entered your realm, but because you have entered the one in which I dwell. This is the reality that the prophets knew that gave them great boldness even when they stood alone against armies."

## The Deadly Trap

I then looked out over the carnage below, and the slowly retreating demonic army. Behind me more of the glorious warriors were constantly taking their places on the mountain. I knew there was now enough to attack and destroy what was left of this enemy horde. "Not yet," said Wisdom. "Look over there." I looked in the direction in which he was pointing, but had to shield my eyes from the glory emanating from my own armor to see anything. Then I caught a glimpse of movement in a valley.

I could not make out what I was seeing, because the glory being emitted from my armor made it difficult to see into the darkness. I asked Wisdom to give me something to cover my armor with so I could see it. He then gave me a very plain mantel to put on. "What is this?" I inquired, a little insulted by its drabness. "Humility," said Wisdom. "You will not be able to see very well without it." Reluctantly I put it on and immediately I saw many things that I could not see before. I looked toward the valley and the movement I had seen. To my astonishment there was an entire division of the enemy horde that was waiting to ambush anyone who ventured from the mountain.

"What army is that?" I asked, "and how did they escape the battle intact?"

"That is Pride," explained Wisdom. "That is the hardest enemy to see after you have been in the glory. Those who refuse to put on this cloak will suffer much at the hands of this most devious enemy."

As I looked back at the mountain I saw many of the glorious warriors crossing the plain to attack the remnants of the enemy horde. None of them were wearing the cloaks of humility and they had not seen the enemy that was ready to attack them from their rear. I started to run out to stop them, but Wisdom restrained me. "You cannot stop this," he said. "Only the soldiers who wear this cloak will recognize your authority. Come with me. There is something else that you must see before you can help lead in the great battle that is to come."

## The Foundation of Glory

Wisdom led me down the mountain to the very lowest level, which was named "Salvation." "You think that this is the lowest level," declared Wisdom, "but this is the foundation of the whole mountain. In any journey, the first step is the most important, and it is usually the most difficult. Without 'Salvation' there would be no mountain."

I was appalled by the carnage on this level. Every soldier was very badly wounded, but none of them were dead. Multitudes were barely clinging to the edge. Many seemed ready to fall off at any moment, but none did. Angels were everywhere ministering to the soldiers with such great joy that I asked, "Why are they so happy?"

"These angels have beheld the courage that it took for these to hold on. They may not have gone any further, but neither did they give up. They will soon be healed, and then they will behold the glory of the rest of the mountain, and begin to climb. These will be great warriors for the battle to come."

"But wouldn't they have been better off to climb the mountain with the rest of us?" I protested, seeing their present condition.

"It would have been better for them, but not for you. By staying here they made it easier for you to climb by keeping most of the enemy occupied. Very few from the higher levels ever reached out to help others come to the mountain, but these did. Even when these were barely clinging to the mountain themselves, they would reach out to pull others up. In fact, most of the mighty warriors were led to the mountain by these faithful ones. These are no less heroes than those who made it to the top. They brought great joy to heaven by continually leading others to 'Salvation.' It was for this reason that all the angels in heaven wanted to come to minister to them, but only the most honored were permitted."

Again I felt a terrible shame at my attitude toward these great saints. Many of us scorned them as we climbed to the higher levels. They had made many mistakes during the battle, but they had also displayed more of the Shepherd's heart than the rest of us. The Lord would leave the ninety-nine to go after the one who was lost. These had stayed in the place where they could still reach the lost, and they paid a dear price for it. I, too, wanted to help but did not know where to start.

Wisdom then said, "It is right for you to want to help, but you will help most by going on to what you have been called to do. These will all be healed and will quickly climb the mountain. They will join you again in the battle. These are fearless ones who will never retreat before the enemy."

## The Power of Pride

I was thinking how descending the mountain was teaching me as much as climbing it had, when noise from the battlefield drew my attention. By now there were thousands of the mighty warriors who had crossed the plain to attack the remnant of the enemy horde. The enemy was fleeing in all directions, except for the one division, Pride. Completely undetected, it had marched right up to the rear of the advancing warriors, and was about to release a hail of arrows. It was then that I noticed the mighty warriors had no armor on their backsides—they were totally exposed and vulnerable to what was about to hit them.

Wisdom then remarked, "You have taught that there was no armor for the backside, which meant that you were vulnerable if you ran from the enemy. However, you never saw how it made you vulnerable if you advanced in pride."

I could only nod my acknowledgment. It was too late to do anything, and it was unbearable to watch, but Wisdom said that I must. To my amazement, when the arrows of pride struck the warriors they did not even notice. However, the enemy kept shooting. The warriors were bleeding and getting weaker fast but would not acknowledge it. Soon they were too weak to hold up their shields and swords, and cast them down, declaring that they did not need them anymore. Then they started taking off their armor, saying it was not needed anymore either.

Then another enemy division appeared and moved up swiftly. It was called Strong Delusion. They released a hail of arrows that all hit their mark. I then watched as just a few of the demons of delusion led off this once great army of glorious warriors. They were taken to different prison camps, each named after a different doctrine of demons. I was astounded at how this great company of the righteous had been so utterly defeated, and they still did not even know what had hit them. "How could those who were so strong, who have been all the way to the top of the mountain, who have seen the Lord as they have, be so vulnerable?" I blurted out.

"Pride is the hardest enemy to see, and it always sneaks up behind you," Wisdom lamented. "In some ways, those who have been to the greatest heights are in the greatest danger of falling. You must always remember that in this life you can fall at any time from any level. 'Take heed when you think you stand, lest you fall.' When you think you are the least vulnerable to falling is in fact when you are the most vulnerable. Most men fall right after a great victory."

## Wisdom for the Battle

"How can we keep from being attacked like this?" I asked.

"Stay close to me, inquire of the Lord before making any major decisions, and keep that mantle on, and the enemy will never be able to blindside you as he did those."

I looked at my mantle. It looked so plain and insignificant. I felt that it made me look more like a homeless person than a warrior. Wisdom responded as if I had been speaking out loud, "The Lord is closer to the homeless than to princes. You only have true strength to the degree that you walk in the grace of God, and 'He gives His grace to the humble.' No enemy weapon can penetrate this mantle, because nothing can overpower His grace. As long as you wear this mantle you are safe from this kind of attack."

I then started to look up to see how many warriors were still on the mountain. I was shocked to see how few there were. I then noticed that they all had on the same mantle of humility. "How did that happen?" I inquired.

"When they saw the battle you just witnessed, they all came to me for help, and I gave them their mantles," Wisdom replied.

"But I thought you were with me that whole time?"

"I am with all who go forth to do the will of the Father," Wisdom answered.

"You're the Lord!" I cried.

"Yes," He answered. "I told you that I would never leave you or forsake you. I am with all of My warriors just as I am with you. I will be to you whatever you need to accomplish My will, and you have needed wisdom." Then He vanished.

## Rank in the Kingdom

I was left standing in the midst of the great company of angels who were ministering to the wounded on the level of "Salvation." As I began to walk past these angels, they bowed to one knee and showed me the greatest respect. I finally asked one of them why they did this, as even the smallest was much more powerful than I was. "Because of the mantle," he replied. "That is the highest rank in the kingdom."

"This is just a plain mantle," I protested.

"No!" the angel protested. "You are clothed in the grace of God. There is no greater power than that!"

"But there are thousands of us all wearing the same mantle. How could it represent rank?"

"You are the dread champions, the sons and daughters of the King. He wore the same mantle when He walked on this earth. As long as you are clothed in that there is no power in heaven or earth that can stand before you. Everyone in heaven and hell recognizes that mantle. We are His servants, but He abides in you, and you are clothed in His grace."

Somehow I knew if I had not been wearing the mantle, and if my glorious armor had been exposed, that the angel's statement, and their behavior toward me, could have really fed my pride. It was simply impossible to feel prideful or arrogant while wearing such a drab, plain, cloak. However, my confidence in the mantle was growing fast.

## The Return of the Eagles

Then on the horizon I saw a great white cloud approaching. Hope arose in me just by seeing it. It actually filled the atmosphere with hope just as the sun rising chases away the darkness of night. As it grew closer I recognized the great white eagles that had flown from the Tree of Life. They began landing on the mountain, taking their place on every level beside the companies of warriors.

I carefully and respectfully approached the eagle who had landed near me because his presence was so awesome. When he looked at me with his penetrating eyes, I knew I could hide nothing from him. His eyes were so fierce and resolute that I trembled as chills ran through me just looking at them. Before I could even ask, he answered me.

"You want to know who we are. We are the hidden prophets who have been kept for this hour. We are the eyes of those who have been given the divinely powerful weapons. We have been shown all that the Lord is doing, and all that the

enemy is planning against you. We have scoured the earth and together we know all that needs to be known for the battle."

"Did you not see the battle that just took place?" I asked with as much irritation as I dared to express. "Couldn't you have helped those warriors that were just taken captive?"

"Yes. We saw it all, and we could have helped if they had wanted it. But our help would have been to restrain them. We can only fight in the battles that the Father commands, and we can only help those who believe in us. Only those who receive us as who we are, the prophets, can receive the prophet's reward, or the benefit of our service. Those who were ambushed did not yet have the mantle that you are wearing, and those who do not have that mantle cannot understand who we are. We all need each other, including these here who are still wounded, and many others who you do not yet know."

## The Heart of the Eagle

By talking to the eagle I started very quickly to think like the eagle. After this short discussion I could see into the eagle's heart and know him like he knew me. The eagle recognized this.

"You have some of our gifts," the eagle noted, "though they are not very well developed. You have not used them much. I am here to awaken these gifts in many of you, and to teach you to use them. In this way our communication will be sure. It must be sure or we will all suffer many unnecessary losses, not to mention missing many great opportunities for victory."

"Where did you just come from?" I asked.

"We eat snakes," the eagle replied. "The enemy is bread for us. Our sustenance comes from doing the Father's will, which is to destroy the works of the devil. Every snake that we eat helps to increase our vision. Every stronghold of the enemy that we tear down, strengthens us so we can soar higher and stay in the air longer. We have just come from a feast, devouring the serpents of shame who have bound many of your brothers and sisters. They will be here soon. They are coming with the eagles we left behind to help them find the way, and to protect them from the enemy's counterattacks."

These eagles were very sure of themselves, but not cocky. They knew who they were, what they were called to do. They also knew us and they knew the future. Their confidence was reassuring to me, but even more so to the wounded that were still lying all around us. Those who had recently been too weak to talk were actually sitting up listening to my conversation with the eagle. They looked at him like a lost child would look to his parent who had just found him.

## The Wind of the Spirit

When the eagle looked upon the wounded his countenance changed as well. In place of the fierce resolution I had stood before, toward the wounded he was like a soft, compassionate old grandfather. The eagle opened his wings and began to gently flap them, stirring up a cool refreshing breeze that flowed over the wounded. It was not like any other breeze I had ever felt before. With each breath I felt I was gaining strength and

clarity of mind. Soon the wounded were standing and worshiping God with a sincerity that brought tears to my eyes. Again I felt a profound shame at having scorned those who stayed on this level. They had seemed so weak and foolish to those of us who were ascending the mountain, but they had endured much more than we had and remained faithful. God had kept them and they loved Him with a great love.

I looked up at the mountain; all of the eagles were gently flapping their wings. Everyone on the mountain was being refreshed by the breeze they were stirring up, and everyone on the mountain was beginning to worship the Lord. At first there was some discord between the worship that was coming from the different levels, but after a time everyone on every level was singing in perfect harmony. Never on earth had I heard anything that beautiful. I never wanted it to end. Soon I recognized it as the same worship that we had known in the Garden, but now it sounded even more full and rich. I knew that it was because we were worshiping in the very presence of our enemies, in the midst of such darkness and evil that surrounded the mountain, that it seemed so much more beautiful.

I do not know whether this worship lasted hours, days, or minutes, but eventually the eagles stopped flapping their wings and it stopped. "Why did you stop?" I asked the eagle that I had been talking to.

"Because they are now whole," he replied, indicating the wounded who were now all standing and appeared to be in perfect condition. "True worship can heal any wound," he added.

"Please do it again," I begged.

"We will do this many times, but it is not for us to decide when. The breeze that you felt was the Holy Spirit. He directs us; we do not direct Him. He has healed the wounded and begun to bring about the unity that is required for the battles ahead. True worship also pours the precious oil upon the Head, Jesus, which then flows down over the entire body, making us one with Him and each other. No one who becomes one with Him will remain wounded or unclean. His blood is pure life, and it flows when we are joined to Him. When we are joined to Him we are also joined to the rest of the body, so that His blood flows through all. Is that not how you heal a wound to your body, by closing the wound so that the blood can flow to the wounded member to bring regeneration? When a part of His body is wounded, we must join in unity with that part until it is fully restored. We are all one in Him."

The euphoria from the worship was still prevailing so that this little teaching seemed to be the most profound that I had ever heard, even though I had known it and taught it myself before. When the Holy Spirit moved every word seemed glorious, regardless of how elementary it was. It also filled me with so much love that I wanted to hug everyone, including the fierce old eagles. Then, like a jolt, I remembered the mighty warriors who had just been captured. The eagle sensed this but did not say anything. He just watched me intently. Finally, I spoke up; "Can we recover those who were just lost?"

## The Wounded Heart of the King

"Yes. It is right for you to feel what you do," the eagle finally said. "We are not complete, and our worship is not complete, until the whole body is restored. Even in the most glorious worship, even in the very presence of the King, we will all feel this emptiness until all are one, because our King also feels it. We all grieve for our brothers in bondage, but we grieve even more for the heart of our King. Just as you love all of your children, but would be grieved for the one that was sick or wounded, He too loves all of His children, but the wounded and oppressed have most of His attention now. For His sake we must not quit until all have been recovered. As long as any are wounded, He is wounded."

## Faith That Moves Mountains

Sitting down by the eagle, I thought deeply about what he said. Finally I asked, "I know that Wisdom now speaks to me through you, because I hear His voice when you speak. I was so sure of myself before that last battle, but I was almost carried away with the same presumption that they were carried away with, and could very easily have been captured with them if Wisdom had not stopped me. I was going out of hatred for the enemy more than wanting to set my brothers free, though that was part of my motive. Since first coming to this mountain, and fighting in the great battle, I now think that most of the right things I did, I did for the wrong reasons, and many of the wrong things I did, I had good motives for. The more I learn, the more unsure of myself I feel."

"You must have been with Wisdom a long time," the eagle responded.

"He was with me a long time before I began to recognize Him, but I am afraid that most of that time I was resisting Him. Somehow I now know that I am still lacking something very important, something that I must have before I go into battle again, but I do not know what it is."

The great eagle's eyes became more penetrating than I had ever seen them as he responded, "You also know the voice of Wisdom when He speaks to you in your own heart. You are learning well because you have the mantle. What you are feeling now is the true faith."

"Faith!" I shot back. "I'm talking about serious doubts."

"You are wise to doubt yourself. But true faith depends on God, not yourself, and not your faith. You are close to the kind of faith that can move this mountain, and move it must. It is time to carry it to places that it has not gone to before. However, you are right. You are still lacking something very important. You must yet have a great revelation of the King. Even though you have climbed to the top of the mountain, and received from every truth along the way, and even though you have stood in the Garden of God, tasted of His unconditional love, and have seen His Son many times now, you still only understand a part of the whole counsel of God, and that only superficially."

I knew that this was so true that it was very comforting to hear it. "I have judged so many people and so many situations wrongly. Wisdom has saved my life many times now, but the voice of Wisdom is still a very small voice within me, and the clamor of my own thoughts and feelings are still far too loud. I hear Wisdom speaking through you much louder than I hear Him in my own heart, so I know I must stay very close to you."

"We are here because you need us," the eagle replied. "We are also here because we need you. You have been given gifts that I do not have, and I have been given gifts that you do not have. You have experienced things that I have not experienced, and I have experienced things that you have not known. The eagles have been given to you until the end, and you have been given to us. I will be very close to you for a time, and then you must receive other eagles in my place. Every eagle is different. It is together that we have been given to know the secrets of the Lord, not individually."

## The Doors of Truth

The eagle then lifted up from the rock on which he had been perched, and soared over to the edge of the level on which we stood. "Come," he said. As I approached him I saw steps that led down to the very base of the mountain. There was a small door.

"Why have I not seen this before?" I asked.

"When you first came to the mountain you did not stay on this level long enough to look around," he answered.

"How did you know that? Were you here when I first came to the mountain?"

"I would have known if I had not been here, because all who miss this door do so for the same reason, but in fact I was here," he responded. "I was one of the soldiers you so quickly passed on your way up the mountain."

It was then that I recognized the eagle as a man whom I had met soon after my conversion, whom I had actually had a few conversations with. He continued, "I wanted badly to follow you then. I had been on this level for so long that I needed a change. I just could not leave all of the lost souls that I was still trying to lead here. When I finally committed myself to doing the Lord's will, whether it was to stay or go, Wisdom appeared to me and showed me this door. He said it was a shortcut to the top. That is how I got to the top before you did, and was changed into an eagle."

I then remembered that I had seen doors like this on a couple of the levels. I had even peeked into a couple of them and remember how amazed I had been at what I saw. I did not venture into any of them very far, because I was so focused on the battle and trying to get to the top of the mountain. "Could I have entered any of those doors and gone right to the top?" I asked.

"It is not quite that easy," the eagle remarked, seeming a little irritated. "In every door there are passage ways, one of which leads to the top." Obviously knowing my next question, he continued. "The other ones lead to the other levels on the mountain. The Father designed each so that everyone would choose the one that their level of maturity dictated that they needed."

"Incredible! How did He do that?" I thought to myself, but the eagle heard my thoughts.

"It was very simple," continued the eagle as if I had spoken my thoughts out loud. "Spiritual maturity is always determined by the willingness of one to sacrifice their own desires for the interests of the kingdom or for the sake of others."

I was carefully noting all that was said. I somehow knew that I must enter the door before me, and that it would be wise for me to learn all that I could from someone who had been there before and had obviously chosen the right door to the top.

"I did not go directly to the top, and neither have I met anyone who has," the eagle continued. "But I went there much faster than most because I had learned so much about self-sacrifice while fighting here on the level of 'Salvation.' I have shown you this door because you wear the mantle and would have found it anyway, but the time is short and I am here to help you mature quickly. There are doors on every level, and every one leads to treasures that are beyond your comprehension. They cannot be acquired physically, but every treasure that you hold in your hands you will be able to carry on in your heart. Your heart is meant to be the treasure house of God. By the time you reach the top again, your heart will contain treasures more valuable than all of the treasures of the whole earth. They will never be taken from you, but they are yours for eternity, because you are God's. Go quickly. The storm clouds are now gathering, and the great battle is near."

"Will you go with me?" I pleaded.

"No," he responded. "This is where I now belong. I have much to do to help these who were wounded. But I will see you here again. You will meet many of my brother and sister eagles before you return, and they will be able to help you better than I at the place where you meet them."

## The Treasures of Heaven

I already loved that eagle so much that I could hardly stand to leave him. I was glad to know I would see him again. Now the door was drawing me like a magnet. I opened it and entered. The glory that I beheld was so stunning that I immediately fell to my knees. The gold, silver and precious stones were far more beautiful than anything I had ever seen on the earth. The room was so large that it seemed to be without end. The floor was silver, the pillars gold, and the ceiling was pure diamond that emitted every color I had ever known and many that I had not known. Angels without number were everywhere, dressed in different robes and uniforms that were of no earthly origin.

As I began to walk through the room, the angels all bowed in salute. One stepped forward and welcomed me by name. He explained that I could go anywhere and see anything that I wanted in the room. Nothing was withheld from those who came through the door.

I could not even speak I was so overwhelmed by the beauty. I finally remarked that this was even more beautiful than the Garden had been. Surprised, the angel responded, "This is the Garden! This is one of the rooms in your Father's house. We are your servants."

As I walked, a great company of angels followed me. I turned and asked the leader why they were following. "Because of the mantle," he said. "We have been given to you, to serve you here and in the battle to come."

I did not know what to do with the angels so I just continued walking. I was attracted to a large blue stone that appeared to have the sun and clouds within it. When I touched it the same feelings flooded over me as when I ate the fruit of the Tree of Life. I felt energy, great mental clarity, and love for everyone and everything being magnified. I started to behold the glory of the Lord. The longer I touched the stone the more the glory increased. I never wanted to take my hand off of the stone, but the glory became so intense that I had to look away.

Then my eyes fell on a beautiful green stone. "What does that one have in it?" I asked the angel standing nearby.

"All of these stones are the treasures of salvation. You are now touching the heavenly realm, and that one is the restoration of life," he continued.

As I touched the green stone I began to see the earth in rich and spectacular colors. They grew in richness the longer I had my hand on the stone, and my love for all that I saw grew. Then I began to see a harmony between all living things on a level that I had never seen before. Then I began to see the glory of the Lord in the creation. It began to grow until again I had to turn away because of the intensity.

Then I realized that I had no idea how long I had been there. I did know that my comprehension of God and His universe had grown substantially by just touching these two stones, and there were many, many more. There was more in that one room than a person could have absorbed in a whole lifetime. "How many more rooms are there?" I asked the angel.

"There are rooms like this on every level of the mountain that you climbed."

"How can one ever experience all that is in just one of these rooms, much less all of them?" I asked.

"You have forever to do this. The treasures contained in the most basic truths of the Lord Jesus are enough to last for many of your present lifetimes. No man can know all that there is to know about any of them in just one life, but you must take what you need and keep proceeding toward your destiny."

I started thinking about the impending battle again, and the warriors who had been captured. It was not a pleasant thought in such a glorious place, but I knew I would have forever to come back to this room, and only had a short time to find my way back to the top of the mountain, and then back to the battle front again.

I turned back to the angel. "You must help me find the door that leads to the top."

The angel looked perplexed. "We are your servants," he responded, "but you must lead us. This whole mountain is a mystery to us. We all desired to look into this great mystery, but after we leave this room that we have come to know just a little about, we will be learning even more than you."

"Do you know where all of the doors are?" I asked.

"Yes. But we do not know where they lead. There are some that look very inviting, and some that are plain, and some that are actually repulsive. One is even terrible."

"In this place there are doors that are repulsive?" I asked in disbelief. "And one that is *terrible*? How can that be?"

"We do not know, but I can show it to you," he responded.

"Please do," I said.

We walked for quite a time, passing treasures unspeakable, all of which I had great difficulty not stopping to touch. There were also many doors, with different biblical truths over each one. When the angel had called them "inviting" I felt that he had quite understated their appeal. I badly wanted to go through each one, but my curiosity about the "terrible door" kept me moving. Then I saw it. "Terrible" had also been an understatement. Fear gripped me so that it took my breath away.

## Grace and Truth

I turned away from that door and retreated fast. There was a beautiful red stone nearby, which I almost lunged at to lay my hands on it. Immediately I was in the Garden of Gethsemane beholding the Lord in prayer. The agony I beheld was even more terrible than the door I had just seen. Shocked, I jerked my hand away from the stone and fell to the floor in exhaustion. I badly wanted to return to the blue or green stones, but I had to regather my energy and sense of direction. The angels were quickly all around me serving me. I was given a drink that began to revive me. Soon I was feeling well enough to stand and begin walking back to the other stones. However, the recurring vision of the Lord praying compelled me to stop.

"What was that back there?" I asked.

"When you touch the stones we are able to see a little of what you see, and feel a little of what you feel," said the angel. "We know that all of these stones are great treasures, and all of the revelations they contain are priceless. We beheld for a moment the agony of the Lord before His crucifixion, and we felt briefly what He felt that terrible night. It is hard for us to understand how our God could ever suffer like that. It makes us appreciate much more what an honor it is to serve you whom He did it for."

The angels' words were like lightning bolts straight to my soul. I had fought in the great battle. I had climbed to the top of the mountain. I had become so familiar with the spiritual realm that I hardly noticed angels any more, and I could speak on nearly equal terms with the great eagles, yet I could not bear to share in even a moment of the sufferings of My King without wanting to flee to a more pleasurable experience. "I should not be here," I almost shouted. "I, more than anyone, deserve to be a prisoner of the evil one!"

"Sir," the angel said almost shyly. "We understand that no one is here because they deserve it. You are here because you were chosen before the foundation of the world for a purpose. We do not know what your purpose is, but we know that it is very great for everyone on this mountain."

"Thank you. You are most helpful. My emotions are being greatly stretched by this place, and they have tended to overcome my understanding. You are right. No one is here because they are worthy. Truly, the higher we climb on this mountain, the more unworthy we are to be there, and the more grace we need to stay there. How did I ever make it to the top the first time?"

"Grace," my angel responded.

"If you want to help me," I then said, "please keep repeating that word to me whenever you see me in confusion or despair. That word I am coming to understand better than any other, and it always brings great illumination to my soul."

"Now I must go back to the red stone. I know now that is the greatest treasure in this room, and I must not leave until I am carrying that treasure in my heart," I said with more resolution in my words than I felt in my heart at that time, but I nevertheless knew that it was true.

## The Truth of Grace

The time that I spent at the red stone was the most painful that I have ever experienced. Many times I simply could not take any more but had to withdraw my hand. Several times I went back to the blue or green stones to rejuvenate my soul before I returned. It was extremely hard to return to the red stone each time, but my love and appreciation for the Lord was growing through this more than anything I had ever learned or experienced.

Finally, when the presence of the Father departed from Jesus on the cross, I could not stand it anymore. I quit. I could tell that the angels, who were also experiencing what I was, were in full agreement. The willpower to touch the stone again simply was not in me anymore. I did not even feel like going back to the blue stone. I just laid on the floor weeping over what the Lord had gone through. I also wept because I knew that I had deserted Him just like His disciples. I failed Him when He needed me the most, just like they did.

After what seemed like several days, I opened my eyes. Another eagle was standing beside me. In front of him were three stones, one blue, one green, and one red. "Eat them," he said. When I did, my whole being was renewed, and both a great joy and great soberness flooded my soul.

When I stood up, I caught sight of the same three stones set into the handle of my sword, and then on each of my shoulders. "These are now yours forever," the eagle said. "They cannot be taken from you, and you cannot lose them."

"But I did not finish this last one," I protested.

"Christ alone will ever finish that test," he replied. "You have done well, but you must go on now."

"Where to?" I asked.

"You must decide, but with the time getting shorter I will suggest that you try

> *The treasures contained in the most basic truths of the Lord Jesus are enough to last for many of your present lifetimes.*

to get to the top soon," the eagle replied as he departed in an obvious hurry.

Then I remembered the doors. I immediately started toward the doors that had been so appealing. When I reached the first one it simply did not appeal to me anymore. Then I went to another, and it felt the same. "Something seems to have changed," I remarked out loud.

"You have changed," the entire troop of angels replied at once. I turned to look at them and was amazed at how much they had changed. They no longer had the naive look they had before, but were now more regal and wise-looking than any of the angels I had seen. I knew they reflected what had also taken place in me, but I now felt uncomfortable just thinking about myself.

"I ask for your counsel," I said to the leader.

"Listen to your heart," he said. "That is where these great truths now abide."

"I have never been able to trust my own heart," I responded. "It is subject to so many delusions, deceptions, and selfish ambitions, that it is hard to even hear the Lord speaking to me above the clamor of it."

"Sir, with the red stone now in your heart, I do not believe that will continue to be the case," the leader offered with uncharacteristic confidence. I leaned against the wall, thinking that the eagle was not here when I needed him the most. He had been this way before and would know which door to choose. But I knew he would not come back, and I knew that it was right that I choose. As I pondered, the "terrible door" was the only one that I could think of. Out of curiosity I decided to go back and look at it. I had departed from it so fast the first time that I had not even noticed which truth it represented.

As I approached it I could feel the fear welling up inside of me, but not nearly as bad as the first time. In great contrast to the others, it was very dark around this door, and I had to get very close to read the truth over it. Mildly surprised, I read THE JUDGMENT SEAT OF CHRIST. "Why is this truth so fearful?" I asked aloud, knowing that the angels would not answer me. As I looked at it I knew that it was the one I should go through.

"There are many reasons that it is fearful," the familiar voice of the eagle responded.

"I'm very glad you came back," I replied. "Have I made a bad choice?"

"No! You have chosen well. This door will take you back to the top of the mountain faster than any other. It is fearful because the greatest fear in the creation has its source through that door—the holy fear of God. The greatest wisdom that men can know in this life, or in the life to come, are found through those doors, but very few will go through them."

"But why is this door so dark?" I asked.

"The light of these doors reflect the attention that the church is presently giving to the truths behind them. The truth behind that door is one of the most neglected of these times, but it is one of the most important. You will understand when you enter. The greatest authority that men can receive will only be entrusted to those who will go through this door. When you see Christ Jesus sitting on this throne, you too will be prepared to sit with Him on it."

"Then this door would not be so dark and forbidding if we had just given more attention to this truth?"

"That is correct. If men knew the glory that is revealed behind that door, it would be one of the most brilliant," the eagle lamented. "However, it is still a difficult door to pass through. I was told to return and encourage you because you will soon need it. You will see a greater glory, but also a greater terror than you have ever known. But know that because you have chosen the difficult way now, it will be much easier for you later. Because you are willing to face this hard truth now, you will not suffer loss later. Many love to know His kindness, but very few are willing to know His severity. If you do not know both you will always be in danger of deception and a fall from His great grace."

"I know that I would never come here if I had not spent the time that I did at the red stone. How could I keep trying to take the easy way when that is so contrary to the nature of the Lord?"

*"But now you have chosen, so go quickly. Another great battle is about to begin, and you are needed at the front."*

To be continued . . . ∎

# WITH ALL THY GETTING, GET UNCTION!

by
Leonard Ravenhill

INTERCESSION

*All Scriptures KJV unless otherwise indicated.*

The Cinderella of the church of today is the prayer meeting. This handmaid of the Lord is unloved and unwooed because she is not dripping with the pearls of intellectualism, nor glamorous with the silks of philosophy; neither is she enchanting with the tiara of psychology. She wears the homespun clothing of sincerity and humility and so is not afraid to kneel!

The offense of prayer is that it does not essentially tie in to mental efficiency (that is not to say that prayer is a partner to mental sloth; in these days efficiency is at a premium). Prayer is conditioned by one thing alone, and that is spirituality. One does not need to be spiritual to preach, that is, to make and deliver sermons of homiletical perfection and exegetical exactitude. By a combination of memory, knowledge, ambition, personality, plus well-lined bookshelves, self-confidence and a sense of having arrived—brother, the pulpit is yours almost anywhere these days. Preaching of the type mentioned affects men; prayer affects God. Preaching affects time; prayer affects eternity. The pulpit can be a shop window to display our talents; the closet speaks death to display.

The tragedy of this late hour is that we have too many dead men in the pulpits giving out too many *dead* sermons to too many dead people. Oh! the horror of it. There is a strange thing that I have seen "under the sun" even in fundamentalist circles; it is preaching without unction. What is unction? I hardly know. But I know what it is not (or at least I know when it is not upon my own soul). Preaching without unction kills instead of giving life. The unction-less preacher is a savor of death unto death. The Word does not live unless the unction is upon the preacher. *Preacher, with all thy getting—get unction.*

Brethren, we could well manage to be half as intellectual (of the modern pseudo kind) if we were twice as spiritual. Preaching is a spiritual business. A sermon born in the head reaches the head; a sermon born in the heart reaches the heart. Under God, a spiritual preacher will produce spiritually-minded people. Unction is not a gentle dove beating her wings against the bars outside of the preacher's soul; rather, she must be pursued and won. Unction cannot be learned, only earned—by prayer. Unction is God's knighthood for the soldier-preacher who has wrestled in prayer and gained the victory. Victory is not won in the pulpit by firing intellectual bullets or wisecracks, but in the prayer closet; it is won or lost before the preacher's foot enters the pulpit. Unction is like dynamite. Unction comes not by the bishop's hands, neither does it mildew when the preacher is cast into prison. Unction will pierce and percolate; it will sweeten and soften. When the hammer of logic and the fire of human zeal fail to open the stony heart, unction will succeed.

What a fever of church building there is just now! Yet without unctionized preachers, these altars will never see anxious penitents. Suppose that we saw fishing boats, with the latest in radar equipment and fishing gear, launched month after month and put out to sea only to return without a catch—what excuse would we take for this barrenness? Yet thousands of churches see empty altars week after week and year after year, and cover this sterile situation by misapplying the Scripture, **"My word . . . shall not return unto me void"** **(Isaiah 55:11).** (Incidentally, this seems to be one of the very few texts that the dispensationalists forgot to tell us was written to the Jews!)

The ugly fact is that altar fires are either out or burning very low. The prayer meeting is dead or dying. By our attitude to prayer we tell God that what was begun in the Spirit we can finish in the flesh. What church ever asks its candidating ministers what time they spend in prayer? Yet ministers who do not spend two hours a day in prayer are not worth a dime a dozen, degrees or no degrees.

Away with this palsied, powerless preaching, which is unmoving because it was born in a tomb instead of a womb, and nourished in a fireless, prayerless soul. We may preach and perish, but we cannot pray and perish. If God called us to the ministry, then, dear brethren, I contend that we should get unctionized. *With all thy getting—get unction*, lest barren altars be the badge of our unctionless intellectualism. ∎

---

**Leonard Ravenhill** was born in 1907 in Yorkshire, England and became one of England's foremost outdoor evangelists. Throughout his more than 60 years of ministry he was a strong voice to the church, exhorting Christians toward repentance, revival, intercession and holiness. Leonard authored several bestselling books, including *A Treasury of Prayer, Revival Praying, Revival God's Way, Why Revival Tarries, America is Too Young to Die, Sodom Had No Bible* and *Tried and Transfigured*. These and many of his other works are available through your local bookstore. The above article was excerpted from *Why Revival Tarries*, published by **Bethany House.**

# IN MY FATHER'S ARMS

by

## Ken Helser

*One cannot paint into a picture that which is not in oneself.*

— **Agnes Sanford**

Can you hear the cry of the children: "Show us the Father!"? I do. "But, Lord," I asked, "how do I answer that cry?" He showed me when on ocean's shore Andy lifted little Luke high on his shoulder. Suddenly it was all there: the pier's weathered crosses, the sea tossed rebellion of youth, and, a father's arms. If a picture speaks a thousand words, please allow me to share a few words about the picture.

I was determined that my little girl was not going to date until she was forty, but somewhere around the ripe old age of sixteen, she and mama broke me. I did insist though that the boy had to be a Christian. "But how will I know, Daddy?" Dustie would whine. She didn't like my answer. "Let me talk to him and I'll find out." Needless to say, she didn't date often.

E. V. Hill once said, "You can't make race horses out of mules; you gotta match 'em up." I must confess that I tried, but it was God that matched up Dustie and Andy and after dating for five years, they were married. They quickly grew as one, and the mathematics of one plus one in love soon made THREE! Dustie was pregnant.

We all were excited, but not as much as Andy's dad. Mr. Gregson was hunting for toys even before Dustie started showing. He also took it the hardest when, after the third month, she lost the child. Then there was a second miscarriage. By the third pregnancy everyone held their breath and excitement, until the seventh month when Dustie was looking well-rounded. Her approaching due date had all of us jumping every time the phone rang. "Is it Dustie? Is it Dustie?" One morning the phone did ring, but it wasn't the call we expected. Two weeks before the due date, Andy's father died suddenly of a heart attack.

The day of the funeral the church was packed. Andy had asked if he could share a few words about his dad. He stood behind the pulpit that overlooked the flag-draped casket. "Jesus, you gotta help me do this," he prayed. The Holy Spirit took over.

"When I was 7 or so, my dad, like all dads to their little boys, was larger than life, my hero. I remember waiting all day for him to come home. He would throw me up in the air so that I could 'walk' around the house on the ceiling and let me pick the change covered in mortar dust out of his pockets. Dad was a brick mason and his hands were huge, thick, and rough as sandpaper. He never wore gloves. His hands could be so gentle or, when I asked for it, like a brick on my backside. When I was a child, my dad was like God.

"I began to work with him on Saturday jobs in my teens. By then, I had become so much smarter and wiser than he. How could a man who had lived so long know so little about life? We had our battles and things changed between us. He didn't know how to fix it and I was too concerned about myself to care. I worked with Dad every summer, beginning the summer before I went off to The Citadel. Over the next six years he and I spent a lot of time together on construction sites. They say that working for your dad is tough. That is a serious understatement. So Dad was no longer God; he became the old man.

"Something had happened, though, by the time I graduated from college. Dad and my uncle threw a graduation party. Dad didn't embarrass me at all! In fact, the poem he wrote to me and recited in front of everyone was clever, even funny, the highlight of the party. I had secretly respected him for some time. His honesty, integrity and humility were so rare. I was, and still am, in awe of Dad's character. I can't remember how many jobs he made almost nothing on because he worked so cheaply. He often infuriated me by tearing down work that was fine but just didn't meet his impossibly high standards. Dad's price quote on a job never changed, even when the customer forgot to tell us about a 'minor' addition to the work or a situation developed that forced him to incur unplanned expenses.

"I never once heard him complain about sacrifices that his family, job or country asked of him. He worked so hard and had so little yet I can only hope one day to have a portion of the peace and faith that he had in his relationship with God. My pain is how long its taken for me to see that my dad isn't God or the old man. Today my father is my friend."

There wasn't a dry eye in the church when he finished. Everyone's thoughts turned toward their own fathers. I prayed that I would never forget the moment and that I could somehow communicate to others its truth.

"In My Father's Arms" was given by God in answer to that prayer. The Lord enabled me to paint over four hundred hours and never lose the joy of the revelation that in the wilderness years of youth, when we are deceived in thinking that we are wise and in control, God carried us . . . "as a father carries his son." ■

# IN MY FATHER'S ARMS

In my Father's arms I was lifted high
Close to His heart, I could touch the sky
For dad was like God and could silence wave's roar
And tame all my fears on ocean's shore
For nothing could touch me or cause me harm
As a child I was safe in my Father's arms.

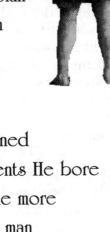

From my Father's arms the years brought a day
When far from His heart I wandered away
Dad was not God but just the old man
I mocked his wisdom and questioned his plan
A proud adolescent with a mind of his own
My Father's arms I'd completely outgrown.

To my Father's arms born-again I returned
Back to His heart from the wilderness learned
That pier's weathered crosses were moments He bore
My sea-tossed rebellion when He loved me more
For now I'm a father, he's not God or old man
In my Father's arms He became my best friend.

by Ken Helser

YOU'LL HEAR THE CANDID TESTIMONIES OF:

GLEN CAMPBELL; "TRAIN UP A CHILD IN THE WAY HE SHOULD GO, AND WHEN HE GETS OLD HE WON'T DEPART FROM IT. THAT'S MY STORY."

RICKY SKAGGS; "I WAS LIKE A KID WITH A BUTCHER KNIFE, LASHING OUT AT WHATEVER WENT AGAINST GOD'S WORD AND THAT'S NOT MY PLACE. MY PLACE IS TO TELL THEM ABOUT JESUS CHRIST."

THE GATLIN BROTHERS; "WHEN LARRY CHECKED INTO THE CARE UNIT IN DECEMBER OF '84 IT MADE US ALL LOOK AT OURSELVES AND REPRIORITIZE OUR LIVES."

SOUNDTRACK AVAILABLE ON:

COLUMBIA

NOT AVAILABLE IN STORES

## Silent Witness
### A TRIBUTE TO COUNTRY'S GOSPEL LEGACY

AN ORIGINAL MUSIC VIDEO COLLECTION OF GOSPEL FAVORITES AND POWERFUL TESTIMONIES OF FAITH FROM:

GLEN CAMPBELL  TAMMY WYNETTE  MARTY RAYBON  SAWYER BROWN
THE GATLIN BROTHERS  RICKY SKAGGS
MARTY STUART WITH JERRY AND TAMMY SULLIVAN  JOHNNY CASH

**HERE'S WHAT VIEWERS ARE SAYING ABOUT THE POWERFUL TESTIMONIES AND MUSIC VIDEOS:**

"I BELIEVE THIS MAY BE THE TOOL GOD USES TO REACH MY LOST LOVED ONES."
-MARIA GREEN, LIBERTY, MO

"I BELIEVE THIS VIDEO CAN SPEAK TO HEARTS THAT MORE ORGANIZED RELIGION HAS MISSED. IT TOUCHED MY HEART."
-MRS. J.B. MUSGROVE, GRAPELAND, TX

"SILENT WITNESS HAS QUICKLY BECOME KNOWN AS ONE OF THE MOST UNIQUE AND POWERFUL TOOLS FOR EDIFYING CHRISTIANS, OR TOUCHING NON-CHRISTIANS THAT HAS EVER BEEN PRODUCED. THE QUALITY OF MUSIC BY THESE TOP ARTISTS, COMBINED WITH THEIR TESTIMONIES IS LIKE 'APPLES OF GOLD IN SETTINGS OF SILVER.'"
-RICK JOYNER, MorningStar PUBLICATIONS

RESOUNDINGLY ENDORSED AS A POWERFUL EVANGELISTIC TOOL BY MINISTRIES ACROSS THE UNITED STATES. FROM TBN TO DR. JERRY FALWELL

HOME VIDEO $29.95 + $4.00 S&H
CD $14.99 + $2.50 S&H
CASSETTE $9.99 + $2.50 S&H
MASTERCARD AND VISA ACCEPTED

TO ORDER CALL: 1-800-942-2645
OR SEND YOUR CHECK TO:
SILENT WITNESS
P.O. BOX 1591
JACKSONVILLE, NC 28541

Florida residents add sales tax
© 1994 RAINMAKER FILMS

"SOMETIMES A SONG CAN SOFTEN THE HEART LIKE NOTHING ELSE."

## Ken Helser Ministries

## ABOUT THE ARTIST

Ken Helser is multitalented—a writer, painter, speaker, song writer and singer. But he would rather be known as one for whom Christ died and chose to reveal his love.

Once the Lord spoke to Ken, saying: "The key to creativity is being free from fear," and "The key to discipline is desire."

Never having had any formal training in art, Ken is thrilled to have several of his watercolor paintings featured on the cover of *The Morning Star Journal.*

His desire is to encourage others to find God's creative purpose in their own lives, "to become all that He had in mind when He chose to reveal His Son to you."

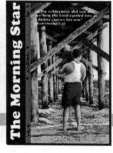

For a free brochure or information, call or write:

**KEN HELSER MINISTRIES**

4221 Beckerdite Rd.
Sophia, NC 27350
910-861-1407
Fax 910-861-7034

# GRACE TRAINING CENTER
## OF KANSAS CITY
### (A MINISTRY OF METRO VINEYARD FELLOWSHIP)

**Sam Storms, Ph.D.**
**PRESIDENT**

*Grace Training Center is committed to both the <u>centrality of Scripture</u> and the <u>power of the Holy Spirit</u> in the context of the local church. Our goal is to <u>equip men and women</u> for service in God's kingdom by nurturing a biblical harmony between <u>theological integrity</u> and Spirit-empowered <u>passion for Jesus</u>.*

**Mike Bickle**
**DIRECTOR**

- In-depth Biblical Studies
- Cultivating Holy Passion For God
- Ministry In The Power Of The Spirit
- Nurture Of Prophetic Ministry
- Intercession For Revival

- Worship And The Arts
- Leadership Development
- Training In Godly Character
- Cell Group Based Ministry
- Missions & Church Planting Vision

1, 2, AND 3 YEAR STUDY PROGRAMS ◆
INTERNSHIP PROGRAM ◆
LOW TUITION COSTS ◆

**FACULTY**

- Sam Storms, Ph.D.
- Wes Adams, Ph.D.
- Mike Bickle
- Michael Kailus, M.Div.

- Philip Pidgeon, D.Min.
- Jim Goll, B.S.
- Noel Alexander, M.Div.
- Robb Black, M.A.
- George LeBeau, Th.M.

- Tim Gustafson, M.Div.
- Bruce McGregor, M.Div.
- John Enderby, M.Div.
- Paul Baskins, M.Div.

*For a free brochure and more information, call or write*
**Grace Training Center**
**11610 Grandview Rd.**
**Kansas City, MO 64137**
Ph: (816) 765-4282 Fax: (816) 767-1455

# EMMAUS ROAD MINISTRY SCHOOL

## *TRAINING FOR MINISTRY WITH A BURNING HEART*

### Biblical, practical ministry training for adults with teachers like . . .

◆ *Dudley Hall*    ◆ *James Robison*    ◆ *Jack Deere*

◆ *Rick Joyner*    ◆ *Jack Taylor*

◆ *Dennis Peacocke*    ◆ *Doug White*    ◆ *Jim Hylton*

Resident ministry training consisting of two semesters, four hours each day, four days a week. Begin in September or January. Affordable tuition. Dallas/Fort Worth, Texas.

For more information write to:
Emmaus Road Ministry School
P.O. Box 400213
Euless, Texas 76040
(817) 545-0282

# *Living Water* Journal

**One Year Subscription**

(4 Quarterly Issues)

**$10.00** U.S.
**$15.00**
Outside U. S.

Our desire is that God will use us to:

❖ Refine Hearts
❖ Renew Minds
❖ Remake Lives

O ur purpose is to provide prophetic teaching to the believer that will instruct, equip, and further the kingdom of God in their lives. To this end, each quarterly edition of the *Living Water* Journal is a topical study of a principle from the kingdom of God designed to enlighten and challenge the believer.

Send name, address, and payment to:

*Living Water* **Ministries, Inc.**
P.O. Box 4653
Rockford, IL 61110

*"Whosoever believes in me, as the Scripture has said, streams of living water will flow from within him."*

# The Morning Star Fellowship of Ministries

The *MorningStar Fellowship of Ministries* (MFM) was founded to serve three basic parts of the overall vision of *MorningStar*. **First** is the equipping, oversight, and support of ministries related to *Morning-Star*. **Second** is to use the relationship that *MorningStar* has with many different parts of the body of Christ to promote interchange, understanding and friendship between them. The **third** is for the mobilizing of spiritual forces for the sake of the gospel.

For additional information, or to request an application, contact:

**The MorningStar Fellowship of Ministries**
16000 Lancaster Highway
Charlotte, NC 28277
Phone 704-542-9880 • Fax 704-542-5763

*First in the new series . . .*

## "COMBATING SPIRITUAL STRONGHOLDS"

### *Overcoming The Religious Spirit*
by Rick Joyner

Contents include:
- Discerning the Religious Spirit
- Masks of the Religious Spirit
- Twenty-five Warning Signs of a Religious Spirit
- Ten things you can do to get free from the Religious Spirit
- The Jezebel Spirit
- Spiritual Witchcraft
- and more

Catalog No. RJ1-010
ISBN 1-878327-44-5
*Booklet, 36 pages*
Retail: $2.50

MorningStar Price Only $2.00!
(save 20% off retail price)

## Do You Know The Scriptures? The Power Of God?

At *The MorningStar School of Ministry* you will come to both know and experience the Scriptures *and* the power of God. We are committed to the equipping of future Christian leaders with the knowledge and practical experience needed for effective ministry. We are now accepting applications for full- or part-time students in both day and evening classes. Ordination will be made available through *MorningStar Fellowship of Ministries*.

For additional information, or to request an application, contact:

The
MorningStar
School of
Ministry

16000 Lancaster Highway
Charlotte, NC 28277
Phone 704-542-9880
Fax 704-542-5763

*Jesus replied, "Are you not in error because you do not know the Scriptures or the power of God? (Mark 12:24)."*

# John G. Lake

## His Life, His Sermons, His Boldness of Faith

Respected as a father of faith, **John G. Lake**—one of this century's greatest preachers—was an example of a believer sharing God's supernatural love and miracle-working power. Through his refreshing sermons and distinguished lifestyle, Lake revealed insightful answers to modern issues such as racism, dominion and the truth about healing.

Now **Kenneth Copeland Publications** releases the most complete and comprehensive book ever published about John G. Lake. This volume of more than 500 pages includes a stirring biography, historical photos, unaltered sermons—many never before published—and much more. It will show you how bold faith can come alive in any believer who will receive!

For **VISA, MasterCard** or **Discover** orders, call

## 1-800-957-5522

any time. Or, write Kenneth Copeland Ministries, Fort Worth, Texas 76192-0001. Ask for offer **#2113** and enclose **$17.95** (price includes shipping and handling).

**KCP** **Kenneth Copeland Publications**

---

# The MorningStar School of the Spirit

If you are visiting the Charlotte, North Carolina area, consider joining us for a time of worship, teaching and ministry devoted to "...equipping the saints for the work of service" (Ephesians 4:12).

Call the **MorningStar offices** for **meeting times** and **directions** at:

## (704) 542-0278

---

# *You're Invited . . .*

to join us every Sunday morning at 10:00 a.m. for a time of worship, praise, teaching and prophetic ministry. Special worship and ministry is provided for children of all ages. We are located at 627 Pressley Road in Charlotte, North Carolina, near the airport and Charlotte Coliseum. Call (704)542-0278 for directions.

MorningStar **FELLOWSHIP**

*The MorningStar*

# Tape of the Month

**You receive a tape each month of the latest message from the minister**

<u>Only</u> **$49.00**/year!

**($65 USD outside US)**

<u>Plus...</u>

**You can add secondary subscriptions for**

<u>Just</u> **$29.00** each!

**($39 USD outside US)**

*For those who are seeking in-depth teaching and prophetic ministry, MorningStar offers a quality and diverse program designed to provide monthly, cutting edge messages that are both edifying and challenging. Also, all subscriptions to our Tape of the Month include a free subscription to* **The MorningStar Prophetic Bulletin** *and a free 12-place tape album.*

## Paul Cain

Paul is recognized around the world as one of the important prophetic voices of our time. Paul's *Tape of the Month* is devoted to challenging the church to the integrity, purity, and power that will be required of those who are called to be a part of the last day ministry.

**Catalog #T2-001**

## Jack Deere

A former professor at the conservative Dallas Theological Seminary, and author of **Surprised by the Power of the Spirit**, his teachings contain depth and insight, making even the most basic truths come alive with powerful relevance for today.

**Catalog #T3-001**

## Francis Frangipane

Francis has emerged as an important new voice to the body of Christ. His first book, **The Three Battlegrounds**, became an international best-seller. The focus of his *Tape of the Month* is to impart a clear, practical, and Christ-centered vision that casts down strongholds that hinder Christian maturity.

**Catalog #T4-001**

## Rick Joyner

Rick is the editor of **The Morning Star Journal** and the author of several best-selling books. Rick's *Tape of the Month* combines prophetic vision with in-depth teaching, often combined with insightful historical perspectives, for a clear revelation of the last day purposes of the church.

**Catalog #T1-001**

# ORDERING INFORMATION

**MAIL**

Send order and payment to:
**MorningStar Publications**
**Order Department**
**16000 Lancaster Hwy**
**Charlotte, NC 28277**

**PHONE**

**Order Department:**
8:00 a.m. - 8:00 p.m. Mon. - Fri.
(Eastern Time)
**1-800-542-0278**

**FAX**

Fax order form
24 hours a day to:
**1-704-542-0280**